William W. Patton

Spiritual Victory

Thoughts Upon the Higher Christian Life

William W. Patton

Spiritual Victory

Thoughts Upon the Higher Christian Life

ISBN/EAN: 9783337160210

Printed in Europe, USA, Canada, Australia, Japan

Cover: Foto ©Lupo / pixelio.de

More available books at **www.hansebooks.com**

SPIRITUAL VICTORY:

OR,

Thoughts upon the Higher Christian Life.

BY

WILLIAM W. PATTON.

BOSTON:
CONGREGATIONAL PUBLISHING SOCIETY,
CONGREGATIONAL HOUSE,
BEACON STREET.

PREFACE.

THE substance of the following chapters will be recognized by some as having appeared, in another form, in the religious journal which for several years was under the editorial care of the writer. They indicate a main object, which he kept in view while serving Christ and the Church in that capacity, and were originally intended to present Christian duty and privilege in a manner at once discriminating and attractive. The instruction which inquiring souls seemed to gain from them, and the fact that they exhibit certain truths in other than their ordinary aspect, may be a sufficient warrant for their revision and republication in the present form. May the blessing of Him by whose grace "we are more than conquerors through him that loved us," and who "shall bruise Satan under our feet shortly," attend this effort to show his people the methods and the certainty of SPIRITUAL VICTORY!

W. W. P.

CHICAGO, ILL., May 1, 1874.

CONTENTS.

CHAPTER I.
CHRISTIAN LIFE A WARFARE 9

CHAPTER II.
THE VICTORY INSPIRED 18

CHAPTER III.
ASCETICISM IS NOT VICTORY. 27

CHAPTER IV.
THE VICTORY DESCRIBED 36

CHAPTER V.
REALIZING FOR WHOM WE FIGHT 47

CHAPTER VI.
THE CAPTAIN OF OUR SALVATION 55

CHAPTER VII.
THE GREAT ADVERSARY 63

CHAPTER VIII.
A GOSPEL OF VICTORY 74

CHAPTER IX.
VICTORY BY FAITH 84

CHAPTER X.
Philosophy of Faith's Victory 96

CHAPTER XI.
Faith's Habit of Victory 106

CHAPTER XII.
Victory over Evil Habit 115

CHAPTER XIII.
Victory over Physical Habit 125

CHAPTER XIV.
Prayer a Legitimate Weapon 136

CHAPTER XV.
The Weapon Two-edged 147

CHAPTER XVI.
The Weapon Tested 161

CHAPTER XVII.
Victory through Self-Denial 173

CHAPTER XVIII.
Victory through Sorrow 184

CHAPTER XIX.
Victory through Joy 195

CHAPTER XX.
Victory at the Outposts 204

CONTENTS.

CHAPTER XXI.
CONTINUAL VICTORY 213

CHAPTER XXII.
CRISES OF THE CAMPAIGN 221

CHAPTER XXIII.
LEGAL EXPERIENCE A DEFEAT 231

CHAPTER XXIV.
VICTORY OVER PRIDE 245

CHAPTER XXV.
VICTORY OVER ANXIETY 255

CHAPTER XXVI.
VICTORY OVER SENSITIVENESS 265

CHAPTER XXVII.
VICTORY IN DETAIL 274

CHAPTER XXVIII.
VICTORY ON THE FIELD OF BUSINESS 284

CHAPTER XXIX.
VICTORY ACCORDING TO LAW 296

CHAPTER XXX.
THE FINAL VICTORY 304

SPIRITUAL VICTORY.

CHAPTER I.

CHRISTIAN LIFE A WARFARE.

EVERY one must have noticed the use which the Bible makes of the figure of war as setting forth our earthly experience. Probably nothing could more forcibly appeal to our imagination, and give us an idea of the difficulties which must be overcome in reaching purity and heaven. What is our natural, unregenerate condition but one of subjection? We are ruled over by our conqueror, the devil, "are taken captive by him at his will," and, like ancient captives in war, are sold into slavery,—"sold under sin," and "brought into captivity to the law of sin which is in our members." We are delivered from this thraldom by Jesus Christ, the "Captain of our salvation," who "hath led captivity captive." He enrols us in his army, tells us to "fight the good fight of faith," to "endure hardness as a good soldier of Jesus Christ," and to remember that "no man that warreth entangleth himself with the affairs of this life, that he may please him who hath chosen him to be a soldier." We are warned against "our adversary the devil," and told that if we "resist the devil, he will flee from us." It was this conception which led Paul to write to the Ephesians, "Take unto you the whole armor of God. . . . Stand, therefore, having your loins girt about with truth, and having on the breastplate of righteousness, and your feet shod with the preparation of the gospel of peace; above all, taking the shield of faith, whereby ye shall be able to quench all the fiery darts of the wicked [one]; and take the helmet of salvation, and the sword of the Spirit, which is the word of God." And so, a little before his death, on reviewing his Christian life, he said, "I have fought a good fight." And for us all, as at once a hint and an encouragement, the promise is unto "him that overcometh."

And how readily our prayers accept this figure, as setting forth our daily experience! We confess and deplore our weakness, our defeats, our fleeing before the enemy. We tell of the open assaults and cunning stratagems of Satan.

We supplicate divine aid in the conflict. We pray that we may have courage for life's battles, and that the Church may become "terrible as an army with banners." And when we sing of the Christian life we fall into the same strain. We say to others,—

> "Brethren, while we sojourn here,
> Fight we must, but should not fear."

We call upon our souls to "gird the gospel armor on," and to think that "glittering robes for conquerors wait." We chide ourselves by the question, "Am I a soldier of the cross?" And we sing, "Sure I must fight if I would reign." Would we animate fellow-saints to fidelity, we break out in the words,—

> "Stand up, stand up for Jesus,
> Ye soldiers of the cross!"

As we think of spiritual danger we exclaim, " My soul, be on thy guard ! " And, in our desire for the world's salvation, we utter the wish, —

> " Now be the gospel banner
> In every land unfurled."

And so we go through life, talking to ourselves and to one another as if we were in a war; as most truly we are.

But our conception is ordinarily far below the reality. We need to rouse our imagination to a more vivid picturing of spiritual facts, till we feel in the inmost soul how actual the conflict is, how sore the strife, how lasting the struggle, and yet how sure the victory. The new life is an entrance on a campaign which ends not till we pass through the gates of pearl. " The kingdom of heaven suffereth violence, and the violent take it by force." All the evil tendencies and habits of the previous life of sin fight against the purpose of the convert to live for God.

He carries out his purpose; but it is by bearing down all inward opposition, in the name of Christ, and "crucifying the old man with the affections and lusts." His first victory is over himself. Then he learns that he is surrounded by spiritual foes, and that the very atmosphere about his soul is full of rebellion against God. He is situated much as a citizen would have been during the late war, who should have returned to loyalty in the Southern States. He lives in a revolted world, and yet tries to be loyal to his King. He is not quite alone; there are others like-minded; but the majority is with the ungodly. He is tempted to join the multitude, and to live as does the world at large. At least, may he not be allowed to keep his sentiments to himself, and avoid conflict with the opinions and practices of his neighbors? If he may not relinquish the service of Christ, may he not make a truce with the world? No: Christ's enemies are also his enemies; and he must "have no fellowship with the unfruitful works of darkness, but rather reprove them." Victory for the truth, and not ease for himself, must be his care. A soldier has only to fight: none but the general can make a truce.

But the worst of all is, that his chief antagonist is invisible, and is therefore difficult to manage, and apt to be forgotten. Indeed, one of Satan's masterpieces of success is, to make men disbelieve his existence, and to explain the numerous and explicit declarations of Scripture as figures of rhetoric, or as references to current superstitions. Alas! that there should be a diabolically inspired exegesis of Scripture. But none the less do we "wrestle against principalities, against powers, against the rulers of the darkness of this world, against spiritual wickedness in high places." Oh for divine direction in this war! Where shall we learn how the battles are to be fought, and the victories to be won? In the closet, studying the Bible, and gaining a previous inspiration on our knees; so that we shall be "more than conquerors through Him that hath loved us," and who shall "bruise Satan under our feet shortly."

"Pass on from strength to strength :
Faint not, nor yield.
With girded loins press on ; the goal is near :
With ready sword fight God's great battle here :
Win thou the field ! "

CHAPTER II.

THE VICTORY INSPIRED.

BATTLES have usually been fought under an inspiring influence. With some it has been that of patriotism, with others love of glory, with others desire of booty, with still others revenge. Mere discipline will indeed accomplish wonders, and must constitute, ordinarily, the basis of success; but the effective power of an army is immensely increased when an ardor possesses it which impels to action, and despises fear. The French have owed many of their military successes to their dash and enthusiasm. No doubt the legions of old Rome gained an inspiration from their national pride and repeated successes, and were victorious because they fought under the assurance that they were invincible. Not seldom, in the heroic days, devotion to an idolized leader was all the inspiration needed to move men to deeds of greatest daring.

There must be an inspiration in order to the victory of the Christian over his spiritual enemies. Holiness is no drudgery, though its habit, when formed, answers to the effect of military discipline. It is a joyous ardor in the service of God. It is a loving zeal for Christ, the Captain of our salvation. Love is always an inspiration. How it works in the mother, to do and dare in behalf of her offspring! How it impels the betrothed and the wedded to act and to suffer for dear companions! Who can describe what Jesus did for us under the inspiration of love? And who can measure the answering power of affection begotten by the thought in the soul of the saint? When men wondered at the labors and sacrifices of Paul, and suggested that he must be beside himself, he explained the mystery by the simple and all-sufficient words, "The love of Christ constraineth us." That was his inspiration.

The actual power of inspiration, in this as in other respects, is the Holy Spirit. At the time of the betrayal and crucifixion, the apostolic band was timid in the extreme. They meant well, and talked courageously; but, when actual danger came, they all forsook their Master, and fled. Six weeks later they faced the multitude and the rulers, accused them of murdering the Messiah, and welcomed stripes and imprisonment. During the interval they had received the baptism of the Spirit, which wrought such faith and hope, such love and courage, such zeal and enthusiasm, as to overcome natural fear, and to make that a joy which once had been a dread. This is the office of the blessed Spirit, — to inspire every Christian for his life-work, to be an inward power in the soul, to be a substitute to the Church for the inspiring visible presence of Jesus himself till at the end of the world he shall come in his glorious second advent. Such was the Master's promise: "I will pray the Father, and he shall give you another Comforter, that he may abide with you forever." "He dwelleth with you, and shall be in you." "He will guide you into all truth." Because this is our hope, Paul beseeches us by "the love of the Spirit," cautions us to "quench not the Spirit," assures us that "the fruit of the Spirit is in all goodness and righteousness and truth," and bids us to be "praying always with all prayer and supplication in the Spirit." True saints are those who "walk not after the flesh, but after the Spirit," who "mind the things of the Spirit," and in whom "the Spirit of God dwelleth." He is in us "the Spirit of adoption," and "beareth witness with our spirit, that we are the children of God."

There is a sense of inspiration in the very knowledge of the fact that we have the perpetual presence of such wisdom, power, and love. The idea of a divine Comforter ever within, — the revealer of truth, the bestower of grace, the inworking spiritual life of the soul, as it were the Lord Jesus become an invisible guardian, — this of itself ennobles and animates the believer, when it fully possesses the mind. It brings God near, and makes him as an atmosphere to the soul, a source of perpetual health and vigor. Faith in such boundless aid near at hand, in a spiritual potency which accompanies us at every step, is natural and easy; and thus the childlike, trustful spirit is begotten, which is the secret of all progress in piety. God afar off is not wholly an inoperative idea; but what is its inspiring power compared with that of God at hand, God within us? This we realize as we come to a proper conception of the presence and indwelling of the Comforter. "Hereby know we that we dwell in him, and he in us, because he hath given us of his Spirit."

But, while the Spirit works, in ways unknown to us, among the very springs of thought and feeling, strengthening, healing, vivifying, comforting, we are made conscious of inspirations from him as "the Spirit of truth," by the light poured upon the Scriptures, and by the quickening effect upon the mind of fresh views of the facts and doctrines of the Bible. One reason of the marvellous change in the apostles on the day of Pentecost lay in the clear and new ideas gained of the meaning of the Old Testament, with reference to the Messiah. Now that they understood why Christ had died, — that it was to atone for sin, and to bring eternal life within the reach of lost men, — they felt joyfully and irresistibly moved to proclaim the fact, and to face all danger in his behalf. And so it is with every Christian. He has the fulfilment of the Master's promise : "When he, the Spirit of truth, is come, . . . he shall glorify me ; for he shall receive of mine, and show it unto you." What we need for victory is the inspiration which comes from an assurance of our riches in Christ ; that through him we "can do all things ;" that he "is of God made unto us wisdom and righteousness and sanctification and redemption ;" so that we are "complete in him, who is the Head of all principality and power." Our prayer and faith should be, that the blessed Spirit would fill us with such a sense of Christ's love in the past and in the present, as shall overcome opposing influences. Then to serve him will be not bondage but liberty; and we shall testify to the truth of his words, "My yoke is easy, and my burden is light." Then every battle will be a victory.

> "All bitterness is from ourselves:
> All sweetness is from Thee.
> Sweet God! forevermore be **Thou**
> **F**ountain and fire in me."

CHAPTER III.

ASCETICISM IS NOT VICTORY.

VICTORY never means fleeing before one's foes. No campaign could be pronounced triumphant which surrendered to the enemy part of the territory in contest. When France made peace with Germany, ceding to the latter Alsace and Lorraine, every Frenchman hung his head. That national act acknowledged a terrible defeat; and not a man on either side thought of calling it a French victory, even if the remainder of the land was thereby saved to France. And so, in our late civil war, had even a single State, Texas or Florida, for instance, been allowed to remain out of the Union, the result would have been recorded in history as an ill success of the Federal forces. The Union claimed every State, from the Atlantic to the Pacific, from the Lakes to the Gulf; and victory meant the complete enforcement of that claim.

And yet asceticism has the presumption to call itself spiritual victory, when it is nothing but signal defeat. It is in the position of a party in court which on a certain point confesses judgment, by ceasing to press its claim. For what is asceticism, but a retiring from the conflict with sin, as to a part of the territory in dispute between God and the world? It is a ceasing to claim and to use for God one part of the body, or one department of life. It is a change of moderation into abstinence, of virtue into inaction, of fight into flight. God has bestowed upon us a wondrously contrived body, with appetites and passions connected with the use of the various senses. This body is not miscalculated in any respect. It has not one superfluous capacity of action, or of enjoyment. Spiritual victory recognizes and insists upon God's right to the use of all; and it succeeds in dispossessing Satan everywhere, and in putting every power to virtuous use. But asceticism, shrinking from such a universal conflict as too difficult and dangerous, recommends the saint to abandon altogether certain uses of the body, to forego utterly certain enjoyments, because temptation — that is, conflict — is connected with them. And it persuades the deluded person who listens to the deceptive plea, that such a surrender of the field is a victory over the world, the flesh, and the devil. Hence, early in the history of the Christian Church, asceticism preached the superior holiness of celibacy over marriage, and actually claimed for the former the virtue of chastity, which as properly belongs to the latter ; for there may be a chaste wife as truly as a chaste virgin. Thus also sprang up the idea of the perpetual virginity of Mary, the mother of Jesus; which has no word of support from Scripture, but rather certain plain intimations to the contrary. Thus was introduced the mischievous rule of celibacy for the clergy ; which made good ecclesiastics, but poor pastors and corrupt men. Thus arose the various orders of monks and nuns, who, contrary to nature and the gospel, withdrew from secular employments and family ties, under the false notion of a higher religious experience. Refusing God's gifts, and contravening the divine plan, were called peculiar piety. Retreating from married life, with whatever it might involve of temptation and discipline, was dignified with the name of conquest of evil. Precisely similar was the mistake as to bodily macerations. Those who would be saints were bidden to practise many and severe fasts, to wear coarse and irritating clothing, to lie upon the ground, the floor, or hard and uncomfortable beds, to keep long vigils, to inflict stripes upon themselves, and to avoid pleasant food. This proceeded upon the false assumption that a comfortable mode of life, if not wrong, was so surrounded by temptation that it should be renounced, to avcid danger to the soul. But where has God said that we are to avoid all danger? And where is the place from which all danger can be excluded? And in what passage is the Bible guilty of the absurdity of calling a retreat a victory?

There is less danger, in these days, that asceticism will take the extreme form just named, though Romanism still flourishes, and ritualism borrows approvingly its repressive exercises. Among spiritual Protestants the temptation is, to listen to the voice of asceticism in so far as to confound various departments of virtuous life and action with "the world" which we are to put beneath our feet. One Christian abandons politics, because "they are so corrupting;" another withdraws from business, because "it makes the mind so worldly;" a third will engage in no amusements, because "they are dissipating;" a fourth will not go into society, and be present at parties, because "they interfere with a devotional frame of mind;" a fifth refuses to enjoy art in its varied forms, or to delight in literature, or to put culture to use, because "self-denial is to be the governing rule of life." It must be admitted that all these things are corrupted by the world, and that Satan has long possessed in them the prevailing influence; but that is no reason why the Christian soldier should flee away from them, and, when he gets to what he considers a safe distance, should turn around and call them hard names, and imagine that such a procedure is a victory. These are necessary departments of life. They belong to human development and a true civilization. They must be appropriated by Christianity, and put to needful use by the Church. To desert the ground, and to leave it to the occupation of the world, the flesh, and the devil, is cowardice and not courage, is treason and not loyalty. Spiritual victory means piety which triumphantly maintains all human relationships, and makes natural but pure use of all innocent activities and enjoyments in every grade of society.

In this as in other respects Jesus was our perfect example. Here he differed from John the Baptist, who was intended to be a sternly-disciplined prophet for peculiar service (as occasionally a saint now is), but who was not set forth as a model for the people to imitate, and who had the good sense not to require his hearers to adopt his life. On the contrary, John exhorted each to abide contentedly in his ordinary occupation, and to purge it from immoralities. But Jesus was to be our example; and so he was no ascetic in his training or life. He was a man of and among the people, — living in their homes, partaking of their good cheer, attending their marriage-feasts, accepting invitations to their dinner-parties, watching with interest and pleasure the sports of the children in the market-places, and casting no frown upon a single needful occupation in secular life, or upon a single innocent enjoyment. Asceticism was not born of his mind or heart. He believed in victories, not in defeats.

> " Make us, by thy transforming grace,
> Dear Saviour, daily more like thee:
> Thy fair example may we trace,
> To teach us what we ought to be."

CHAPTER IV.

THE VICTORY DESCRIBED.

PERHAPS the inspired, victorious Christian life is more often denoted by the word "spirituality" than by any other. One who has risen above the world, and gained a triumph over his soul's enemies, is spoken of as "a spiritual Christian," or as "a spiritually minded" person. Is this language understood? We fear that it is not.

"Spirituality" is a word used with much vagueness of meaning, and not seldom with an included error. Yet one's conception should be clear on such a point: growth in grace demands it, as well as the value of advice to others. Plainly the word indicates an antagonism to carnality and worldliness. Such is its use in the New Testament, where it is placed in opposition to a life devoted to the world, the flesh, and the devil. It refers properly to a state of mind, a disposition of soul, a generic and controlling motive, rather than to single acts, or to mere outward conduct. Yet the mistake is constantly made, of supposing that spirituality pertains to one class of places and pursuits, and worldliness to another. It is not a question of time, place, and occupation, however, but of supreme purpose and devotion. A minister may be worldly at the sacred altar; and a merchant may be spiritual in the marts of commerce. One lady may be carnally-minded at a prayer-meeting, while another is spiritually-minded at Saratoga or Newport.

We may be aided in reaching a definite idea of spirituality, by a reference to the composition of the word; and that, whichever of the two derivations we may prefer. If the reference be to the human spirit, then we are to conceive of an inward religion, a piety which consists not in outward deeds merely, whether these be drudgeries, rites, charities, or penances, but in the affections and purposes of the soul. It is thus a religion of the spirit and not of the body. In our Saviour's time Judaism had become formalism, and worship meant a round of ceremonies. Therefore he said to the woman of Samaria, "The true worshippers shall worship the Father in spirit and in truth: for the Father seeketh such to worship him. God is a Spirit: and they that worship him must worship in spirit and in truth." Heart-homage is the only real homage. Bent knees are not necessarily devotion. What is the attitude of the spirit toward God? that is the only pertinent question The error of Judaism, which counted the Pharisees peculiarly religious because they spent much time in fasting, repeating prayers, and attending to other ceremonies, is very commonly entertained in the Romish Church to-day, where those are called "the religious" who devote themselves to certain ecclesiastical and devotional duties, as monks, nuns, and members of various orders. But spirituality is a state of mind which is enjoined upon all, which is possible to all, which denotes the victory of every true soldier of the cross, and which one carries with him everywhere, and takes into all his pursuits and pleasures. It is what it claims to be,—a *spirit* of love to God, of consecration to Christ, of devotion to the highest interests of the soul. This spirit may lead to manifold duties of worship, of business, of study, of recreation, as the necessities of the day and hour may require. The outward acts will differ widely : they will be grave and gay, important and trivial, directed Godward and man-ward, referring to time and eternity, to body and soul ; but they will nevertheless flow from one inward fountain. Thus spirituality will be seen to consist *not in the things done, but in the spirit with which they are done.* Some men promote a revival with less spirituality than that with which others pursue secular business, or engage in innocent pleasures.

The same truth comes to light if we connect the word with the Holy Spirit, which the usage of Paul in the eighth chapter of Romans would justify. Thus we read, "To be carnally-minded is death; but to be spiritually-minded is life and peace," which more literally translated is, "The minding of the flesh is death; but the minding of the Spirit is life and peace." This accords with the previous verse: "They that are after the flesh do mind the things of the flesh; but they that are after the Spirit, the things of the Spirit." Through all the connected passage the apostle is speaking of the sanctifying influence of the Holy Spirit. His idea of spirituality is, that the soul should be enlightened, guided, and purified by the Holy Spirit. Hence he writes to the Galatians, "Walk in the Spirit, and ye shall not fulfil the lusts of the flesh," — ye shall gain a perpetual victory over temptation. This affirms no limitation of outward service. One place may be as holy as another; and all action done under the leading of the Spirit is equally accepted of God. There is no necessary part of life which may not be inspired by the divine Spirit, whether it be work or play, social converse or public worship. We read that Jesus, after his baptism and temptation in the wilderness, was "filled with the Spirit;" and yet the first place at which we find him is the wedding in Cana; and he was as spiritual there as he was subsequently at the grave of Lazarus. No man has a right to affirm that Paul was less spiritual when making tents than when preaching the gospel. Sometimes it requires more grace to work with one's hands at the bidding of Providence, than it does to speak in public in behalf of a religious life, or in defence of Christian doctrine. Even in the Old Testament we are told that the skilful artist Bezaleel was "filled with the Spirit of God, in understanding and in knowledge and in all manner of workmanship, and to devise curious works, to work in gold and in silver and in brass and in the cutting of stones, to set them, and in the carving of wood, to make any manner of cunning work." Can any one doubt that in faithfully following this Spirit-guidance in the construction of the tabernacle, Bezaleel was as religiously occupied as were the priests and Levites in waiting at the altar, or as was Moses himself in delivering the divine law to the people?

As God has planned out our lives in the circumstances in which we act, with the existing demands for labor, social intercourse, and recreation, as well as for worship and religious instruction, his Spirit, if duly sought, will be with us equally in the whole round of life's activities. As we need him in all, he will fail us in none. We may take the blessed Comforter with us everywhere, and may with a pure conscience enjoy his sanctifying influences in all that we do. The completely developed life of the civilized world is yet to be inspired by him, that the victory of grace may be universal.

This common-sense and Scriptural view will save us from the self-deception of supposing that we are spiritual because we talk and busy ourselves about technically religious matters, and also from the cant and censoriousness of inculcating, even with bitterness, a spirituality which we misconceive. To be true to God always, and to find him everywhere; to live ever by faith in Christ Jesus; to be simple, innocent, natural, and loving in all relationships; to be filled with the Holy Ghost; to rise easily and spontaneously from fact to truth, from nature to God, from the human to the divine; to accept with the same spirit of consecration and obedience whatever seems to lie in the order of Providence for us to do, whether it be private or public, little or great, secular or ecclesiastical, work or play, — is what we mean by spirituality. This is the true victory, in which the saint overcomes the world, the flesh, and the Devil.

"Finish, then, thy new creation:
Pure, unspotted may we be:
Let us see our whole salvation
Perfectly secured by Thee."

CHAPTER V.

REALIZING FOR WHOM WE FIGHT.

THE battle is the Lord's, not only as to its decision, but as to its object. He is our King. We fight not for ourselves simply, but as his loyal subjects. There is a rebellion against his authority: we ourselves once were rebels. Penitently returning to our allegiance, and mercifully pardoned, we grasp our weapons to maintain the rights of God in his own universe. The conflict begins within, — in ridding ourselves of the delusions of sin, in recovering from insensibility to divine things, in acquiring faith in the unseen. Our king is invisible; and hence a real difficulty in life, an inability to realize the presence and love of God, and to respond with answering affection, is not unusual. It is a frequent defect of religious life, that it is ethical more than personal in its aims, legal rather than loving in its spirit. It has regard to an abstract idea of right rather than to God ; and it is a burden on the conscience rather than a joy of the soul. It consequently lacks warmth and tenderness, liberty and inspiration.

To realize God, — can that be difficult? Yes, in its true, full sense. In childhood it may have puzzled us somewhat, to read, in the eleventh of Hebrews, what seemed a mere truism, "He that cometh to God must believe that he is, and that he is a rewarder of them that diligently seek him." "Why, everybody believes that," we said. We know better now. Even in the intellectual sense, multitudes persuade themselves that God is not separable from his universe, and has no such providential agency, or coming tribunal, as will insure reward to his worshippers and servants. "Every man his own God," says the pantheist; while the less hardy philosophizer affirms that God has left every man to take care of himself as best he can in the established system of things. Worldliness, too, brings a man to the same unbelief by its practical exclusion of God from one's thoughts and plans.

The moral atmosphere of the world does not favor impressions of God on the soul; and it requires something more than to read "Paley's Evidences," or other volume of proof of the Divine existence, to bring home to us in full force the idea that God is. Even a genuine spiritual conversion only initiates this necessary experience, — only plants the seed of God, as it were, in the soul. That seed must be cultivated by all the thoughts and acts which present God to the mind in his living, loving personality. Habitual prayer — prayer which not only often seeks the closet, but goes with us in mental ejaculations all the day long — has great efficacy in this respect, especially when joined with a conscious putting-forth of faith to take hold of the divine promises as actual sources of aid. Praise similarly operates when much used. Blessed is the mind which is full of precious hymns, and the tongue which sings them every hour! Through these gateways God comes into the soul as a welcome presence of power and love.

It is a law of mind, that objects cease to impress in proportion to the withdrawal of attention. A man may be so excited in a battle, as not to know that he has received a wound; and a man may be so excited in the pursuit of earthly pleasure or gain, as not to realize that there is a God. One writes at his desk, absorbed in thought. The clock on the wall above his head strikes each hour with noisy clang: yet he hears no sound. Why? Because just then the clock has no relation to his will. But let him purpose to take the train at half-past four; and, with the knowledge on his part that it will require thirty minutes to reach the station, let that clock strike four; and see how instantly he drops pen, leaps up, seizes hat and overcoat, and rushes from the office! The morning rising-bell is rung in the house at the bedroom door. The man who purposes to heed it, anxious to begin the day's work, hears the first stroke, and leaps from his couch. The drowsy sleeper who has no purpose to obey its summons, and who, in fact, has disregarded it for days or weeks, and has found its sound becoming fainter each morning, at last ceases to hear it at all. So dies God's voice upon the ear that has no purpose to obey him: so fades God himself out of a mind that has no place for him in its thoughts. He becomes only an article in the creed, an intellectual conclusion, a theological opinion, a customary name. His personality ceases; his providence is discredited; prayer is abandoned, or sinks into a mere form; and religion is reduced to an abstract idea of right, and a social law of morality.

Reverse the process, and you reverse the effect. Bring God once more to the throne, by placing him in the chief purpose of a man, and at once he begins to take on reality. Cultivate the thought of him by worship, and he seems yet more real. Act with direct aim to please him, and every such act makes him stand forth more distinctly. Pray to him much, take him into all your plans, ask his aid in the whole of life, and gradually he becomes a perpetual presence, and the most real of all beings.

Spiritual victory must commence with this clear realization of the fact that we belong to a glorious kingdom, on the throne of which God sits; and that it is for him, and not merely for ourselves, that we fight the battle within and without. The inspiring thought is, that we live to God. "I have set the Lord always before me," said the Psalmist.

"Oh! not in circling depth or height,
  But in the conscious breast,
Present to faith, though veiled from sight, —
  There doth his spirit rest.
Oh! come, thou Presence infinite,
  And make thy creature blest!"

CHAPTER VI.

THE CAPTAIN OF OUR SALVATION.

BUT can we approach no nearer to God than by the vague imagination of an infinite Spirit, whom, by all our searching, we can never find out? Are we not in danger of being lost in immensity, as if we were afloat on a shoreless ocean? Can we not make him seem more real to our humanity, while engaged in this earthly conflict, fighting under his eye? We have dwelt upon the influence of practical irreligion, or neglect of God, in preventing the mind from realizing the Divine personality, presence, and agency. When the will ceases consciously to adjust itself to

God's law and government, and to Christ's salvation, and no communion is kept up with the unseen through prayer, God becomes a dim, far-off being, a mere idea or name, bringing to the soul no warmth of love, or inspiration of thought and act. But when the heart bows to his will, and accepts of his redemption, he seemingly draws near, and becomes real; and that soul, through continued faith, worship, and service, finds him to be an ever-present, loving Father.

Let us bring to the front another Bible thought, which may help one to come to the realization of God as a living person, full of sympathy and love, as well as of wisdom and power. It is a curious and instructive fact, that the same Book which severely condemns idolatry, and all approaches to idolatry, emphasizing that sin as especially fatal to true religion, and as specifically forbidding it in the precepts of the New Testament as it was prohibited by the Decalogue in the Old Testament, yet teaches us that we hold such relations to Christ as must lead us into idolatry unless he be more than man. It is the fundamental fact of Christianity, that we are to accept of Christ as our Lord and Master, because in his person God became incarnate. The marvellous truth is declared, that he was "Son of God," as well as "Son of man;" that he was "the Logos," "the Word" (the uttered communication or the revealer of God), who "in the beginning" "was with God, and was God," and who "was made flesh, and dwelt among us, full of grace and truth." Hence we hear him say of himself, "I and the Father are one;" "He that hath seen me hath seen the Father;" "Believe me, that I am in the Father, and the Father in me." And so Paul testifies, that "in him dwelleth all the fulness of the Godhead bodily: and ye are complete in him, who is the Head of all principality and power," and that in him God was "manifest in the flesh."

When God had thoroughly purged the Jewish mind of all tendency to idolatry, he saw that the way was prepared to reveal his loving personality with an increase of sympathetic power. For it is to be noticed that there is a lack of warmth in the bare idea of one, invisible, absolute God. His infinity and mystery make him so unlike us, and remove him so far from us, that he recedes above the blue ether, or is merged in his general laws. Thus we complain of a certain philosophic chill about Unitarianism, which, in appealing to the reason, fails to touch the heart, and has always shown a lack of practical power. And so Mohammedanism, which based itself on the short creed of one unseen God, and opposed idolatry to the death, has lost any living soul it may have had, and has become a dead body of ceremonialism, with a freezing creed of fatalism.

But evangelical Christianity has its life and power in its warm Pauline conception that "God was in Christ, reconciling the world unto himself;" and in the doctrine of Jesus himself, "I am the Way, the Truth, and the Life: no man cometh unto the Father, but by me."

"Neither knoweth any man the Father, save the Son, and he to whomsoever the Son will reveal him." Therefore we may come to our Saviour as to our condescending and redeeming God, without fear of idolatry, or of provoking the Divine anger by giving to another the honour due only unto God. Kneeling penitently and trustfully at his feet, and putting our fingers with Thomas into the print of the nails, with him we may each exclaim, "My Lord and my God!"

And now, surely, God is brought near, and is made very real. We cannot read the gracious words of Jesus; we cannot in imagination witness his recorded deeds of love; we cannot cease to hear the meaning of the prophetic words concerning the name given him, "They shall call his name Emmanuel, which,

being interpreted, is, GOD WITH US,"—
without feeling that God is no far-off
being, no mere architect or world-
builder, no doubtful mystery back of
Nature's laws, no mere legislator even;
but is the embodiment of purity, tenderness, sympathy, and love. Thus the
name God makes place for the *person*
God, as "manifest in the flesh;" and
the words of John come to us as unfold-
ing a central truth: "No man hath seen
God at any time: the only-begotten Son,
who is in the bosom of the Father, he
hath declared him." If any one, then,
finds it difficult, amid the conflicts of
life, to realize God, and to understand
that he fights under a living Captain, let
him think of Jesus, the God-man, the
point of union of the divine and human,
the Revealer of the Father, "the bright-

ness of his glory, and the express image of his person." Let him believe that through him came out before men and angels God's heart of love; and that whatever he was on earth, in unsullied purity and yet in compassionate regard for sinners, such God in heaven is in infinite degree. Why should God seem unreal to a world into which he came as a quickening personality, as the Spirit-begotten and virgin-born Jesus, the Christ, the past Sacrifice, the present Mediator, the future Judge? No: let us joyfully sing, —

> "Soldiers of Christ, arise,
>   And gird your armor on,
>   Strong in the strength which God supplies
>   Through his eternal Son, —
> Strong in the Lord of hosts,
>   And in his mighty power.
> Who in the strength of Jesus trusts
>   Is more than conqueror."

CHAPTER VII.

THE GREAT ADVERSARY.

THE Christian, as we have seen, fights for God, and under the leadership of Christ as the "Captain of salvation." It is also to be considered that he fights against an opposing kingdom, and resists an adversary of fell intent and of manifold resources. Peter warns us that our "adversary the devil, as a roaring lion, walketh about, seeking whom he may devour." Paul bids us "put on the whole armor of God, that we may be able to stand against the wiles of the devil;" to "resist the devil;" and to labor for sinners, "that they may recover themselves out of the snare of the devil, who are taken captive by him." It would thus seem that we have a powerful personal enemy, whom we are to overcome.

Yet an intelligent layman of the "Liberal" ranks inquired of one lately, whether the orthodox still believe in a personal Devil. He had been shocked by the remark of a friend, after the Chicago fire, who observed that nothing had been to him such a confirmation of his belief in the devil as that event; implying that the devil had wrought the malign destruction. Perhaps his friend was thinking of the case of Job, whose calamities are represented to have been brought upon him by Satan, under Divine permission, as tests of character, to show that his piety was not selfish, — an obedience rendered for benefits received, —

but was disinterested, and could abide the loss of outward good. If the conflagration had come on that city by a similar agency, and for a similar reason, we do not know that any man's moral sense need to have been shocked; but, as such an inspired explanation has not been vouchsafed, it was certainly a rash interpretation, of which complaint was made, and quite unnecessary to account for the facts. That which God permits to take place by natural law, or by human agency, when he could easily have prevented its occurrence, is properly considered to have had a providential ordering; and so we may trace the hand of Providence in the Chicago and the Boston fires, and may easily ascertain the lessons which God would have us learn, without a recourse to Satanic agency.

But there is nothing strange or unreasonable in the orthodox doctrine of a personal devil. There may have been superstition, in former ages, in the use to which the doctrine was often put. The supposed agency of the Devil was connected with all evil acts and with all untoward events, in a way to cause needless alarm, and to minister to the demand for priestly intervention. But such a perversion of the truth in no wise disproves it. The fact of the existence of a leading apostate spirit, the head of the rebellion against God, and the inspiration of anti-Christian effort, lacks neither Scriptural proof nor inherent reasonableness.

The affirmations of Scripture are numerous, clear and uniform. They occur in the Old and in the New Testa-

THE GREAT ADVERSARY. 67

ments. Genesis opens with the account of the tempter in the garden, securing the fall of our first parents ; and the Apocalypse closes with the prediction of his final overthrow and destruction in company with all those who have persistently adhered to his revolt. The intervening books consistently speak of his character, of his direct antagonism to Christ, and of his schemes and influence during the world's history, and warn us against his snares. That the letter of the Bible teaches this, no one pretends to deny ; but some argue that these numerous, varied, and persistent declarations must be interpreted figuratively, as a personification of man's evil tendencies and of the world's spiritual dangers. The objections to admitting such an interpretation are, that it is unnatural, that it is called for by no real exigency, that it is inconsistent with the facts and language in many specific passages, and that it admits a loose principle of explanation by which almost any plain statement of Scripture might be set aside. It is hardly too much to affirm that the same reasoning would resolve the Saviour into a myth, or else into a mere figure of speech representing man's good tendencies and God's spiritual grace. The same spiritualizing pen which goes through the Bible effacing the person of Satan could as easily efface the person of Christ; for in Scripture the two are set over personally against each other, from the fall in Paradise to the scenes of the final judgment.

And on what a slender pretext the denial of this Scriptural fact is based!

In what respect is the idea unreasonable? What absurdity is there in believing that there are other and higher orders of being than men? Did the Creator exhaust his power in producing man? As there are innumerable worlds besides this earth, so there may be numberless rational beings besides the inhabitants of earth. Thus the existence of angels is perfectly credible. But these may differ in moral character: some may be holy, and others apostate. Men have fallen: why not angels? And if angels came into being, not in families of hereditary descent, but by the simultaneous creation of individual spirits, then it is quite conceivable that part of them may have remained holy, when others of the number apostatized; and also that the fall of adult beings may have had peculiarly malignant features and results, and especially in the case of leading minds. We can see, then, no greater absurdity in the idea of multitudes of evil spirits, than in the existence before our eyes of millions upon millions of evil men.

But, if this be true, there is no unreasonableness in the supposition that good and evil spirits are concerned in the events of earthly history. God's universe is a unit: especially must his moral universe be one. It is quite conceivable that the creation and redemption of the human race have such distinct relations to angelic history as greatly to interest both good and evil spirits in the result. We know that men influence each other powerfully towards holiness and towards sin, and that this influence is often unconsciously received. Why, then, in our ignorance of spirit-methods and relations, should we reject the idea that we are acted upon by both classes of spirits, that we receive help from good angels and harm from apostate angels, as the Bible clearly asserts that we do?

Once more: if there be a vast number of evil spirits, acting in antagonism to the gospel, as a "power of darkness," and a "kingdom" of evil, what is there so absurd in the idea that they should have as a head and leader some fallen archangel? Why should Paul's declaration be incredible, that there is a "prince of the power of the air, the spirit that now worketh in the children of disobedience"? Such a belief is natural as well as scriptural. Masses of mind usually act under social influences; and one superior mind guides the rest. The apostacy itself, as an extended rebellion, is best explained on such a supposition. Indeed, we can hardly conceive of its occurrence otherwise than as the influence of a commanding mind, high in station, over those accustomed to confide in him, inducing them to follow him in revolt as before in obedience. And so one can best account for the successive developments of sin in this world, especially in its organic and persistent forms, by the agency of a great organizing leader, who heads the opposition to Christ. We do not see that, in itself, it is any more absurd to believe in the devil as the leader of fallen spirits than in Jefferson Davis as the President of the rebellious Confederacy, or in Napoleon Bonaparte as the imperial leader of the French armies in the wars of Europe.

A belief in this doctrine is important (Paul being witness) as warning the Christian against actual danger, and as giving positiveness to the antagonism between good and evil. Prof. Maurice, with his well-known "Liberal" tendencies, clearly saw this practical fact in religion, and refused to explain away the language of the Bible in this respect. And if there be a personal devil, as held by the orthodox, and as described by the letter of Scripture, what a triumph it must be for him, to persuade men that no such being exists!

> "In the way a thousand snares
> Lie, to take us unawares:
> Satan, with malicious art,
> Watches each unguarded part."

CHAPTER VIII.

A GOSPEL OF VICTORY.

BLESSED be God!—that in Christianity we have a gospel, and not a philosophy; a supernatural grace, and not the mere operation of natural law. Christ is our personal Redeemer, and not simply the teacher of improved ethics. The Holy Ghost is the healing influence to restore sinful souls to health; and they are not left to any legal self-struggles. Thus faith, not works, is the condition of salvation in all its parts,—in the process of sanctification as well as of justification. There is, indeed, a divine philosophy in Christianity: otherwise it would not be the product of the divine reason, nor be the chosen divine method; but we accept and use it not as a discovered philosophy (for as such we know but little of it), but as a revelation to faith of a gracious supernatural power.

Do not many preachers of the gospel lose sight of this truth, and, after beginning in the Spirit, end, like the Galatians, in the flesh? 'From childhood up, we have listened to very much so-called evangelical preaching which dropped out the distinctive gospel characteristic in dealing with the question of victory over sin. Christ was recognized chiefly as a justifying Saviour; and faith had its office almost exclusively in accepting pardon on the ground of his death and intercession. But, when it came to the fight against sin, we were thrown back upon our resolutions, purposes, efforts of will to preserve and to overcome past evil habits, attempts gradually and slowly to form new habits according to the necessary laws of mind. There was, to be sure, a word occasionally uttered, that this must not be undertaken in our own strength, and that God must be asked to aid us; but this truth was left in a general, vague, and but slightly influential form; and all the earnest specific directions and illustrations remanded us to a simple pertinacious endeavor on our own part to overcome evil habits. Indeed, we have listened to a multitude of sermons on this subject — supposed by ministers and hearers to be Christian, because preached from a pulpit, and preceded by a text — which were but an ethical philosophy, pointing out the method of nature in a struggle to get right, and which might have been pronounced by some of the old Grecian or Roman moralists. They reminded us, also, of the purely Judaistic and legal method of seeking sanctification, against which Paul so earnestly contended, and the utter inefficacy of which (as resulting in steady defeat) he set forth so emphatically in the seventh chapter of his Epistle to the Romans. The modern effect of such preaching is as discouraging as the ancient. It brings the earnest striver under perpetual condemnation, and results in one of two opposite effects : either the Christian gropes forward, and struggles on, fettered by a legal bondage, and saddened by the constant failure of his ineffectual resolutions; or else, discouraged, he ceases, to a large extent, to struggle earnestly at all, and allows himself in sundry evil habits which dishonor religion, on the ground that nobody expects to gain a victory over them, they are so inveterate. This reminds us of a sermon preached a few years since, in which the clergyman cautioned his hearers against expecting to make rapid progress in sanctification, telling them that sins were to be slowly overcome, one after another, and reminding them that the fruits which ripen the most slowly last the longest. A hearer thereupon quoted, as a new *moral* proverb, " Soon ripe, soon rotten." Did ever mortal so confound things material and spiritual, or offer to religious sluggards such a convenient defence?

Now, the New-Testament conception

of sanctification is radically different. It looks at every thing in the reverse order, — first God and then man. The effect is primarily a grace and not a work. It is the product of supernatural power, from its initiation at the moment of regeneration, till its completion in the final confirmation of the saint in spotless purity forever. Further still, it is a personal work of the Holy Spirit in each soul, under the promise and mediatorial direction of Christ, and is carried forward in the man by a perpetual Divine presence and action. From this it follows, that, though involving voluntary action, it depends far less upon a conscious will-work, a perpetually renewed conflict between temptation and our resolutions, than it does upon a *habitual act of faith* in Christ, as an ever-present, sanctifying Saviour, and in the Holy Spirit as an abiding power of victory in the soul. By such implicit faith, hourly and momently supplies of spiritual strength are received, and the victory comes as the reward of faith, — as God's response to the soul's sure expectation of triumph, based on his full and free promises. This inward Divine working sometimes manifests itself so suddenly and powerfully, in answer to the faith of a soul previously struggling in a legal bondage of resolutions, that it seems to be a special "baptism of the Holy Ghost," and is so called. Under its influence old habits of sin — such as pride, intemperance, anger, tobacco-bondage, and covetousness, which had resisted years of will-work, and of an attempt by a merely natural process, supplemented by vague prayer, to overthrow them, and gradually to form other habits — give way and dissolve like the snow and ice before the south wind; and the man walks forth in freedom, astonished at the ease with which the newly intensified love of Christ enables him to rise above the power of temptation.

This is the reason that Paul, in the eighth of Romans, describes a *state* of victory, in contrast with the *state* of defeat set forth in the seventh chapter; explaining all in these words (verse 2): "For the law of the Spirit of life in Christ Jesus hath made me free from the law of sin and death;" or free from the law which he had just before mentioned (vii. 21, &c.) as "the law of sin in his members," "a law, that, when I would do good, evil is present with me," and which made him exclaim, "Oh wretched man that I am! who shall deliver me from the body of this death?" The victory was not merely by harder and more persistent struggling, but by receiving, through faith in Christ as a sanctifying as well as a justifying Saviour, the gift of the Spirit. Hence even our efforts are to be put forth in the distinct consciousness of this fact; and we are to "work out our own salvation with fear and trembling," in full confidence of the result; because "it is God that worketh in us, to will and to do of his good pleasure," and not because *our* effort is a philosophical foundation of new and better habits. In this, as in all other respects, "we walk by faith," "looking unto Jesus," "abiding in him," and remembering that "of God are we in Christ Jesus, who of God is made unto us wisdom and righteousness and sanctification and redemption," and that "this is the victory that overcometh the world, even our faith." Paul knew well what advice to give to his Ephesian converts, when, starting from the right end of things, he said, "Above all, taking *the shield of faith*, wherewith ye shall be able to quench all the fiery darts of the wicked." Bless God!—we again say— that in Christianity we have a supernatural power, and not a mere divine law; a gospel grace, and not an ethical philosophy.

> "I cannot rest till in thy blood
> I full redemption have;
> But thou, through whom I come to God,
> Canst to the utmost save."

CHAPTER IX.

VICTORY BY FAITH.

HOW does faith work spiritual victory? A moral philosopher, looking simply at natural laws, and at a human will striving to govern itself by conscience, would easily be stumbled at the idea that sin is to be subdued by faith. Faith in whom, or in what? Faith of what kind? Faith operating by what method? Faith securing what result, — one partial, or complete? one gradual, or sudden? He reasons that there can be but one way of uprooting habits of sin; to wit, that pointed out by natural law, as the result of continuous human striving in the slow and gradual attempt to manufacture a contrary habit. A man must struggle hard, and then harder: he must will to do right, and when he fails must will again more strongly: he must go at his sins with a desperate determination, taking them by the throat with deadly intent: thus he must fight on, and fight through, not discouraged because he makes little or no perceptible progress, but taking this for his life-battle. If the philosopher be also a Christian, he will at times add a word about faith, because the New Testament so often speaks of faith; but he will seldom mean more by it than a general conviction that God will help us in the battle, so that we shall be saved in the end.

Now, while there is a certain truth in this representation, viewed simply on the side of nature and of legal influences, we cannot but think that equally in idea, in method, and in efficacy, it comes far short of the gospel plan of salvation from sin, which operates chiefly by faith. In so saying, we do not mean that a single act of faith will break up all sinful habits, however ancient and inveterate, and will replace them with pure tendencies of equal strength. No man fights the battle of life in a moment, even by the aid of faith. Faith is, indeed, a "shield," "wherewith," as Paul declares, we "may be able to quench all the fiery darts of the wicked [one];" but it does not substitute a single victory for a campaign. But we mean that faith is to be the abiding act, the habitual state of mind, which shall underlie all we think and do, lifting it from a human to place it on a divine foundation. It starts in complete self-despair,—in a conviction of the utter impotency of our resolutions to resist temptation, and to uproot evil habit; and it rests solely on the promised indwelling of the Holy Spirit given by Christ in answer to believing application. Taught by the words of Jesus, "Without me ye can do nothing," with Paul it says, at every breath, "Not that we are sufficient of ourselves to think any thing as of ourselves; but our sufficiency is of God." Its *conscious* act, therefore, is not so much a resolution against sin (which is rather implied) as a perpetual trusting in Christ for grace to keep it from sin moment by moment. Its prompting is, to lean, to confide, to pray, to expect; not in separate, formal exercises (though these occur), but rather in abiding union of soul to Christ, and in constant fellowship with him.

For notice: faith is properly confidence in a person. We *believe* in a truth; but we have *faith* in a person. Therein is the grand peculiarity of the gospel: it does infinitely more than to furnish a new code of moral laws: it reveals a personal Saviour, to *whom* we go in faith for all that we need. This is the first, this is the ever-repeated step in spiritual life, to the very end. Thus John, who writes, "This is the victory which overcometh the world, even our faith," explains the idea, when he says, "Ye are of God, little children, and have overcome them: because greater is *he that is in you*, than he that is in the world." Faith receives Christ instead of Satan into the soul. So also Paul declared, "I can do all things through Christ which strengtheneth me." Hence the victory of faith comes from the confidence that, as we have in Jesus a full and complete Saviour, who is at all times with us, so he will at each moment perfectly supply the spiritual need of the soul which leans wholly upon him. Such a soul, ceasing from its legal struggles (or mere efforts of will under the promptings of conscience), simply makes consecration of itself to Christ, puts itself at Christ's disposal, invites him to possess and work and energize all its faculties, hour by hour, and moment by moment, by the power of the Holy Spirit, and *expects that he will do it*. That expectation he fulfils, so that the saint is able to say, "I am crucified with Christ: nevertheless I live; yet not I, but Christ liveth in me : and the life which I now live in the flesh I live by the faith of the Son of God, who loved me, and gave himself for me."

Into this conscious rest in Christ some enter almost immediately, if they understand their privilege, and are taught that this is the divine method of sanctification. In this way a supernatural grace lifts one far above the weakness of a mere natural effort, and gives the soul an immediate victory, which is as continuous as is the simple faith in a present Christ, and in an inwardly abiding Holy Spirit. Moreover, the ease and certainty of this victory of faith are owing, in part, to a cause which we can understand. In one sense it actually supersedes the conflict which comes from the mere antagonism of conscience and sin, by bringing the man under the inspiring, exalting, entrancing, and absorbing power of a personal love of Christ, before which temptation shrivels as flax in the flame. There is a divine philosophy here : there stands revealed in it a law of mind, as plain and sure as the one that repeated efforts at last work a habit, which is more commonly observed and referred to in the legal method of sanctification. Dr. Chalmers develops it in his famous sermon on "The Expulsive Power of a New Affection." The simple question is, Can the Holy Spirit so reveal Jesus, and so keep him before the mind, that sinful habit shall lose its power and its very opportunity? No law of mind forbids; and the Bible authorizes the expectation.

We once read of a reformed drunkard weeping at the open grave of a good man, and declaring that in that grave all his hopes were to be buried, since nothing had kept him from going back to his cups, but the constant watchfulness and loving persuasion and all-powerful personal influence of him who was now dead. He had lived a reformed life through faith in a good man, who was as an atmosphere around him, and not by dint of mere resolution, or by the slow creation of better habits. When thrown back on these latter influences his will lost its power; and he became once more the victim of strong drink. A man has often been reclaimed by the personal love and presence of his mother or his wife, kindling in him an answering affection, when all other influences have failed. The gospel method of reforming sinners is, so to reveal Christ to them in all his loveliness of character and perfection of work as their Redeemer, that they shall have a sure expectation of victory (which is half the battle), and such an answering love as shall lift them out of the reach of former temptation. This inward experience of a mighty love bearing down the foes of Christ is what secures, by what is often termed the baptism of the Holy Ghost, sudden as well as marvellously complete victories. What could be more sudden than the transformation, by the outpouring of the Spirit at Pentecost, of the timid, trembling disciples into bold preachers of the gospel, ready to submit to martyrdom? The Spirit accomplished at once what the slow law of natural habit would have been years in working. There are many who have gained similar victories after deep thought, earnest prayer, full consecration, and expectant faith; some even in cases where a diseased physical effect aided a sinful habit of mind, as in the use of tobacco and alcohol. Such a sense of Christ's presence and love pervaded their souls, such an assurance of their union in all things with him, such a confidence in his power, such a burning desire to please and glorify him, that temptation in those old forms could not gain access to them. This is the higher life, the victorious experience, the deliverance from the perpetual defeat described in the seventh chapter of the Romans as characteristic of a legal experience, and an entrance upon the triumph of faith unfolded in the eighth chapter.

"Faith shows the precious promise, sealed
　　With the Redeemer's blood,
And helps my feeble hope to rest
　　Upon a faithful God."

CHAPTER X.

THE PHILOSOPHY OF FAITH'S VICTORY.

HAS faith, then, a philosophy? Surely it has, — a philosophy simple and obvious. Why should it not have one? It is in no wise opposed to reason. It could not be, seeing that it is, itself, the highest exercise of reason. For what can be more reasonable than to place implicit confidence in the word of God? When Paul exclaimed, "Let God be true, but every man a liar!" we are quite sure that his intellect spoke as well as his piety, and that the philosopher was as apparent as the saint. A philosopher trusts to a law of nature, that is, to a physical law of God, which he has discovered by observation and reason; believing that it will be maintained in operation, so that one may wisely base his calculations upon it, and order his most important plans by it. What is this but faith in God's natural arrangements and seeming physical pledges? The saint finds a promise in the Bible, a book which stands accredited to his most careful observation and deepest reason, as the word of God; and he, in a like exercise of mind with the philosopher, puts confidence in the divine arrangements and pledge, and shapes his life-plan accordingly. Each uses his reason, weighs evidence, and trusts the Almighty. Each philosophizes; and each exercises faith. That their attention is directed to different personal interests, and to different spheres of the divine activity, does not affect the specfic character of the mental act.

Faith, then, is a genuine philosophy. It accepts Christ on the same ground upon which Sir Isaac Newton accepted the law of gravity. It cannot resist the evidence. A believer is but a spiritual philosopher, though he may never have imagined it. The principle involved was well stated by one, not yet enrolled among earth's so-called philosophers, but who yet spoke from the highest reason: we mean John the Baptist, who said of Jesus, "What he hath seen and heard, that he testifieth," and, "He that hath received His testimony, hath set to his seal that God is true." The disciple of Agassiz or Darwin could do no more in accepting the phenomena and laws of the physical universe is expounded by those skilful observers and acute reasoners, who yet differ so widely in their inferences from the same facts. Let us take an illustrative case of faith's philosophy.

Peter, looking out from his little fishing smack on a stormy night, saw Jesus at a distance, walking on the Sea of Galilee, and was terrified as at a ghost. But Jesus called out, "It is I: be not afraid;" and Peter then, in a characteristic burst of enthusiastic confidence, replied, "Lord, if it be thou, bid me come unto thee on the water," and received the command, "Come." Now, of course, faith would lead him to go, trusting to the Master's power and love. But how about philosophy? Perhaps some one will say that it would have forbidden him to venture, because reason teaches that water cannot be walked upon as is the land. We do not accept the conclusion. Reason told Peter, that, if Jesus could so control nature as to walk on the water, he could enable one of his disciples to do the same; and so he started. But the wise condition of such enabling was faith in the power and willingness of the Master. Peter, after a few steps in the blasts of the terrible gale, allowed his fears to prevail over his faith; which was as great a blunder in philosophy as it was a weakness in piety. And so he began to sink; but, crying to Jesus, was rescued, the Master saying to him, "O thou of little faith! wherefore didst thou doubt?" And equally, from another point of view, might it have been said, "O inconsistent philosopher! why didst thou fear to trust thy reason, which affirmed the perfect ability of the Master to hold thee up?"

And does this not shed light upon the philosophy of holy living, which we have been discussing? To walk in purity through this sinful world is as impossible to "the natural man" as it was naturally for Peter to walk on the stormy Sea of Galilee. But Christ led a pure life in this world, even as he trod securely upon the tempestuous sea; and he is able to impart the Holy Spirit of victory to every believer, even as he could sustain Peter upon the waves. In both cases the effect to be wrought is within the sphere of the supernatural: divine power accomplishes that for which mere human power does not suffice. But the indispensable condition of receiving the divine aid is faith, continuous faith. Peter was not to take slow and painful lessons from Jesus in sea-walking, till he had learned new aqueous laws, and had acquired new marine habits, which in twenty years would enable him to cross the Sea of Galilee. No: he was to take the first step in faith, and the second similarly, and so the third and the fourth; and, if he did not doubt, he could cross the sea the first time: it was simply a question of continuity of firm faith. He exercised his will; he used his feet: but faith alone insured the result. We understand a true evangelical as distinguished from a legal experience in a religious life, to be based on a similar philosophy. It is not a life of resolutions and painful self-operatings to form habits by a gradual law of nature; but it is a life of faith in Christ at each successive moment. The soul acts in varied duties, as Peter took steps on the sea; but it expects the spiritual success only from an indwelling Christ, whose grace flows into the trustful soul without intermission, as support would have been given to Peter all the way from the vessel to the side of Christ, had he conquered his doubts. If faith be present, the success can be as perfect the first as the hundredth time. "We walk by faith," says the apostle, laying down the spiritual philosophy; and, when he gives it the form of personal testimony, it is still the same: "I am crucified with Christ: nevertheless I live; yet not I, but Christ liveth in me: and the life which I now live in the flesh I live by the faith of the Son of God, who loved me, and gave himself for me."

Are there, then, no holy habits formed by the Christian, which gradually become a second nature, and a law of his being? Certainly; but these are the results of the victories gained by faith, and will be rapid in their formation in proportion not to the agony and force of our will-work, but to the continuousness, simplicity, and entireness of our trust in Jesus as a sanctifying Saviour. His is the inward power, the ever-inflowing grace, by which we should fully expect to be kept moment by moment, and thus hour by hour, and day by day. Such faith itself becomes a habit of the soul, and is properly the one all-inclusive spiritual habit, which keeps the heart in peace, and the will in strength. Such is the biblical philosophy of sanctification. With the Christian poet it says, —

"Faith, mighty faith, the promise sees,
And looks to that alone ;
Laughs at impossibilities,
And cries, It shall be done!"

CHAPTER XI.

FAITH'S HABIT OF VICTORY.

FIRST things are usually hard things. One is awkward at them. The fingers of the raw apprentice are all thumbs. The sailor-boy who makes his first voyage seems out of place everywhere, — on deck, aloft, or in the forecastle. The child in its first steps does more falling than walking. A new beginner at any work has to keep his thoughts about him, or he easily forgets the thing to be done, or the way in which it is done: moreover, he does it at all only in a very conscious state of mind, and by distinct acts of will. Did the reader ever learn to play upon the piano-forte? How about those early weeks and months of practice? What attention was needed to find the proper key on the finger-board; then to strike it with precision; then to gain the faculty of using two hands at once, and of seeing simultaneously four parts of the musical score; then to acquire ease, rapidity, and grace of execution! How stiff the fingers were! How the wrist and arm ached! What a desperate purpose was required to produce the sounds! But, after a time, the eye fell into a habit of seeing everything at a glance, and the hand of gliding over the keys by a kind of instinctive movement, which cost no effort. Then it was no task, but a positive pleasure to perform on the instrument.

The religious life has an analogy with this experience in natural things. Though it has faith as its distinctive exercise, and is not thrown upon mere self-exertion and natural law, but receives supernatural grace as its sustaining power, yet the faith must be developed from a germ. "Lord, I believe: help thou my unbelief!" is a confession and prayer which every convert has occasion to offer. This is not because faith itself is difficult to understand, or hard to exercise, as a single act. What can be more simple, even to a child's apprehension, than trust in superior power, wisdom, knowledge, and love? What else is the whole life of childhood? And to trust God ought surely to be far easier than to trust man. Certainly we can have no difficulty in understanding what it is to have faith in God. And when we think of our weakness, ignorance, and sin, and of the divine offer to forgive, enlighten, purify, and strengthen us for Christ's sake, if we yield ourselves fully to him, expecting him to be true to his promise, it ought not to be at all hard thus to rely upon him.

But the trouble arises from this: we have not been accustomed to live by faith. That is an entirely new state of mind. Faith sees only God; and we have been wont, in our life of sin, to see every thing but God. We ruled him out of our minds, of set purpose, till we came no longer to think of him; not even to associate him with things which would seem almost necessarily to suggest him. We put self in his place, acted from self and for self, carried self in thought, pleased self in desire, relied on self in effort. What a revolution it was in the soul, to deny self, to crucify self, to renounce self as either aim or source of power! What a novel act, to look away to God, to feel shut up entirely to him, to put the soul in the simply receptive relation, to depend upon him for pardon of past sin, for purification of heart, for each moment's wisdom and efficiency and victory. Unless we have unusually clear and consistent instruction at this point, we shall make a mixed affair of it, and trust God a little, now and then, here and there, and forget to trust him for all things, at all times. Thus we easily slip out of the new mode of living by trusting, and fall back upon our wills and resolutions. Thereby, stripped of power, we yield to temptation, come under a sense of condemnation, and find a war between conscience and desire, in which our poor craven will takes now the one and then the other side, without gaining any deliverance. And so a long period may elapse without escape from this bondage : and all from a lack of faith.

What is needed is, to come into such a clear conviction of the truth that the soul lives, spiritually, only by faith, that the thoughts shall be exercised chiefly in keeping God before the mind as its all in all. This, which requires at first, from its being an unaccustomed attitude of the soul, a distinct and conscious effort of mind, develops ere long into a delightful mental habit. The Christian comes to associate God with every thing, to see God in every thing, to rely on God for every thing. His thoughts are thus turned into virtual prayers, even when no words of petition are on his lips. He is ever in the expectant, trustful attitude.

It is much as if one had suddenly injured a limb, or suffered a paralysis of it, so as to be incapable of walking without a crutch, or the arm of a friend. But one not in the habit of such dependence would need, at first, to think of it all the time, and would easily forget to lean, and thus would meet with many a fall. Yet in a little time he would acquire the habit, and would then lean upon his support as a matter of course, without conscious thought about it. Our deepest purposes invariably assume this permanent and almost unconscious form. Faith may do so; and, as piety ripens, the soul carries, deep down below all its passing and surface exercises, a calm, steady, perpetual trust in God. This is what we mean by the habit of faith.

The growth of this is the growth of sanctification; for in proportion as the Christian fully trusts his Saviour is he filled with love, and kept from the power of Satan; as John teaches when he says, "Ye are of God, little children, and have overcome them: because greater is he that is in you, than he that is in the world." "And we have known and believed the love that God hath to us. God is love; and he that dwelleth in love dwelleth in God, and God in him. Herein is our love made perfect, that we may have boldness in the day of judgment: because as he is, so are we in this world. There is no fear in love; but perfect love casteth out fear: because fear hath torment. He that feareth is not made perfect in love."

"Happy, Saviour, would I be
If I could but trust in thee! —
Trust thy wisdom me to guide;
Trust thy goodness to provide;
Trust thy saving love and power;
Trust thee every day and hour;

"Trust thy blood to cleanse my soul;
Trust thy grace to make me whole;
Trust thee living, dying, too;
Trust thee all my journey through;
Trust thee till my feet shall be
Planted on the crystal sea."

CHAPTER XII.

VICTORY OVER EVIL HABITS.

THE gospel idea of a victory over sin, by the instrumentality of faith in Christ as an ever-present, sanctifying Saviour, is to many a stumbling-block, because of their conception of the ingrained character of evil habit. To overcome a habit of sin, whether in general or in a specific direction, seems to them necessarily a gradual result, slowly wrought out by a natural law of mind, as holy acts insensibly build up new and opposite habits. We have already said, that, while such a process and result is indeed all that natural reason might teach us to expect, it is not all that the gospel reveals to Christian faith and hope, nor is it all that the experience of the saints gives us ground to expect. The New-Testament doctrine rises above the ethical rules of ancient or modern philosophers, introducing a supernatural element which renders possible spiritual victories which were otherwise hopeless.

Can faith in Christ suddenly destroy, or at least fully suspend, the power of a sinful habit? Is it the best thing we can do, to array our resolutions and struggles against the tyranny of old despotic habits, in a fitful, variable, life-long contest, only expecting sufficient divine aid to prevent our being utterly overwhelmed, and to enable us to persevere in a Christian course? Must the Christian character rise with the slowness of a coral reef in the ocean, and await the deposit of act upon act, till at last a new and holy habit lifts itself above the waves of temptation? Or may we look to Jesus for instant victory, for an immediate rescue, which shall be complete at the time, and as permanent in result as the faith on which it depends? These are questions touching the vitals of Christian experience; and to many they present difficulties past solution.

Well may Faber exclaim, —

> "Yet habits linger in the soul:
> More grace, O Lord! more grace!
> More sweetness from thy loving heart,
> More sunshine from thy face!"

For our own part, we gather courage and hope from such an initial fact as regeneration; which, if it be a fact, seems to be a pledge of all that needs to follow. It is a divine intervention to break the current of sinful forces, and to bring in a restoration of character which is above nature. In effect, it is a victory over the soul's previously unbroken habit of sin: it is a moral revolution, which dethrones Satan and enthrones Christ: it is a new birth: it makes a new man. Regeneration starts one, then, on a higher plane and under a supernatural influence. Surely we may expect, ever after, higher than natural results, — something more than the gradual development of mental laws under human efforts. So sudden and grand a triumph, at the moment of conversion, insured by the Holy Spirit, opens up a succession of new possibilities to the believing soul. If the death-blow is then given to the sin-principle, so that a Christian life starts into being on the instant, it is no stretch of faith into presumption to expect sudden, specific deliverances from the particular tyrannies of sin.

Such deliverances often occur in connection with conversion. Men who have been notorious gamblers, and for whom the card-table has had an irresistible fascination, have suddenly become followers of Christ, and have never touched a card or made a bet thereafter. Libertines, to whom female beauty was a perpetual snare, have been converted instantly to an unbroken purity of life. Drunkards have been reclaimed in revivals of religion, who never subsequently fell, even for a moment. These are instances in which an outward habit has been permanently overcome from the instant of conversion, and a victory has so far been gained continuously over all the remaining inward solicitations to those forms of evil. But what evidence is there of corresponding triumphs where the sinful habit is not physical, but purely mental? What can be expected in the case of anger, impatience, revenge, covetousness, discontent, envy, ambition, and similar tendencies and dispositions?

We heard of an incident not long since, which is in point. A certain lady was of a peculiarly irritable temper; and its unlovely exhibitions caused her, as a professed Christian, the greatest mortification and the deepest grief. She struggled and prayed, she resolved and wept, all apparently in vain. Every purpose was swept away in the excitement of even a slight temptation on this sensitive side, till she despaired of victory. Finally she was urged at a meeting, to confide by simple faith in the power of Christ to keep her, and to make a full-hearted surrender of her entire being to him for that purpose. She embraced the thought with earnestness, and consciously laid her soul in the hands of Jesus, inwardly praying all the way back to her house. This was the more appropriate, as her peculiar trials and temptations were at home; and these she had always declared to be so many, that it was impossible for her to rise above them. Opening the front-door, she saw a domestic violating one of her most explicit rules, by carrying a slop-pail down the front stairs; and, to make the matter worse, the domestic was so alarmed at the sight of her mistress, that she dropped the pail ; and the water flowed down the stairs and over the carpet into the hall. The lady uttered not a word, but whispered over and over, "Jesus, help me! Jesus, help me!" and gained the victory. With entire composure she went in, and from that moment found no difficulty in controlling her before ungovernable temper.

This is by no means an isolated case, and gives us the secret of spiritual victory. Mere prayers and tears, resolutions and struggles, put forth in the legal spirit, avail little but to express grief and penitence, and to keep one in the unrest of defeat, as described in the seventh chapter of the Epistle to the Romans. What is needed is a specific faith in Christ for present and all-sufficient help, — a mind that is expectant of triumph through him. One may dwell with profit on the meaning of the first word in that apostolic precept: "*Reckon* ye also yourselves to be dead indeed unto sin, but alive unto God through Jesus Christ our Lord." It is a great thing to "reckon" upon a given fact, — to count upon it, to base our expectations and plans upon it; especially if it be one of God's redemptive facts, to credit which honors his love and faithfulness. To such an expectant state of soul God responds by an inflowing of divine grace which fills and preserves it. In this way evil habit meets a speedy overthrow, such as mere natural causation would fail to accomplish.

"But, of all the foes we meet,
None so oft mislead our feet,
None betray us into sin,
Like the foes that dwell within.
Yet let nothing spoil our peace :
Christ shall also conquer these."

CHAPTER XIII.

VICTORY OVER PHYSICAL HABIT.

WE continue the subject of the relation of faith in Christ to evil habits, because of its importance and of its obscurity and difficulty. Many who mourn over their bondage to certain forms of sin, which have assumed the character of habits, hastily assume that these are invincible. In support of such an assertion, they relate disheartening experiences. They tell of unsuccessful struggles, oft repeated, but ending invariably in defeat. They resolved to *try* to reform their habit (the use of opium, or of tobacco, or of intoxicating liquor, it may have been); and so they ceased from the favorite indulgence for a few days or weeks. But they felt so miserable without the customary stimulus, that their resolution sooner or later gave way. After two or three such experiments they despaired of victory, and concluded to content themselves with moderation instead of abstinence. It is usually evident in these cases, that, at the outset, they had little faith in their success. They doubted whether they should succeed : they believed, perhaps, that they should not. Yet they were willing, under conscience-pressure, to try. How often that word "try" hides a lack of whole-heartedness, an absence of courage, and a want of genuine faith! It is very deceptive ; for the man thinks it is a word of modesty and humility, indicative of self-distrust, when it really means a wavering cf purpose and a distrust of Christ. Hence, when a spiritual victory is to be won, which is called for by the honor of the Master, and the necessities of his own soul, instead of saying, "By the help of Jesus I will do this thing," he falteringly says, "I will try;" and plainly enough he rather expects to fail. Then, having failed, he pacifies conscience by the thought that he *tried*, and found the effort to be of fruitless. His case is peculiar. He is sorry that he began the evil practice; and he advises his boys (in vain, usually) not to take the first step in that direction; but he is now too old to undo the past, and to form better habits!

And is this the best that Christ can do for such a man? If he were fully trusted to work out deliverance, *could* he not do it? And *would* he not? Suppose the man were to go to Jesus in all directness of speech and in all simplicity of heart, and were to say, "Lord Jesus, if thou wilt, thou canst·make me clean. Deliver me, for the healing of my soul, for the honor of thy name, for the advancement of thy cause. Give me the victory by the power of thy Holy Spirit, in this specific thing. Show that thy grace is sufficient for me in this respect, as it was for Paul in his particular weakness. For that purpose I commit to thee my body and soul, assured that thou wilt make me more than conqueror." Suppose this to be the *believing* application: would the Saviour disappoint that faith, and put it to shame? It seems to us little short of infidelity so to affirm.

We do not know that we ever met with a man who testified that his failure to overcome an evil habit followed such specific consecration and faith. It may have followed penitent tears, deep remorse, sincere resolutions, and sorrowing prayers; and especially it may have followed a half-considered purpose, or a good-natured promise made to a fellow-man. No case, however, is recalled to our memory, in which a Christian has said, "I *trusted* Jesus to carry me through this struggle; I verily *expected* the victory by his grace; I *rested* on his promise: but no deliverance came."

Does any one talk of the unreasonableness of expecting miracles? and does he represent the victory of which we speak as a miracle? We know not that it is any more of a miracle than ordinary answers to prayer; which surely imply a divine intervention in earthly affairs, and in the production of inward and outward effects, in the spiritual and in the physical world. It is not for us to limit the operation of the grace of Christ in a legitimate case, such as is the one under consideration. The most wonderful physical effects are produced by purely mental causes, outside of the sphere of religion and of the appeals of prayer. Health is affected in the way of benefit and injury, the color of the hair is suddenly changed, a bodily appetite is impaired or destroyed, and life itself sometimes is taken, by an experience of joy or of sorrow, of hope or of fear. Neither physicians nor philosophers can resolve the mysterious interrelations of body and spirit. It does not stumble us, therefore, that redemption should be thought equal to all necessary spiritual results with their physical concomitants and conditions. And as to alleged facts, we are content to receive intelligent and credible testimony.

A little tract, by Rev. W. H. Boole, called "The Wonders of Grace," published at the "Water-street Tract Rooms," New York City, adduces many striking cases in point. One is of an officer in a church in New York, who had used tobacco for forty years, making, during that time, many efforts to abandon the practice, but always failing because of the resultant inward gnawing. But he was brought to an act of specific faith in Jesus to save him from the appetite; and now, after several years, he testifies: "From that hour all desire left me; and

I have ever since hated what I once so fondly loved." Another is of a prominent church-member in Brooklyn, N.Y., who had used tobacco for thirty years, and could not endure to be without a cigar in his mouth, and sometimes even rose and smoked in the night. After many failures to overcome the habit, one night, when alone, he cast himself on his Saviour for just this victory; and from that hour was delivered from the desire as well as the outward act, and now wonders that he ever loved the filthy practice. A certain old lady who lived near Westbrook, Conn., aged seventy, was a confirmed opium-eater, and used daily an amount sufficient to kill twenty persons. She was led to see that the habit was a *sin;* and as such she abandoned it with specific application to Christ to save her from it. She was heard, and lived for two years afterwards, free from any desire for that drug. A similar case was that of a carpenter in Brooklyn, N.Y., who, from taking morphine to allay the pain of a fractured leg, fell into its habitual use, till he almost lived upon it for several years after his recovery. He once swallowed, in the presence of several physicians, a dose which it was calculated would destroy the lives of two hundred ordinary men. Not long since he was made to look at this as sin, and tried to break off the habit, abstaining with an alarming re-action, till five physicians declared that death would ensue if he did not resume it. This he did for a year, but then, on a certain Sunday evening, broke off again, casting himself by faith on Christ; from which moment the desire left him, and has never returned, and he has experienced no re-action or other ill effect, but has greatly improved in health.

Such facts, if well authenticated, should encourage the most despairing. We do not see that they are out of analogy with many admitted facts, which are connected with the relations of the body to the mind. Certainly they speak hope to professed Christians, who are insnared by wrong physical habits, and to drunkards and opium-eaters, who seem to be "led captive by Satan at his will." Let no Christian limit the victories of faith within the sphere of redemption from sin.

"Thou, O Christ, art all I want;
More than all in thee I find;
Raire the fallen, cheer the faint,
Heal the sick, and lead the blind.

Just and Holy is thy name :
I am all unrighteousness ;
Vile and full of sin I am :
Thou art full of truth and grace."

CHAPTER XIV.

PRAYER A LEGITIMATE WEAPON.

THE faith which has been urged naturally relies upon prayer, as a legitimate weapon in the spiritual conflict; but the right to use this weapon is called in question by the philosophers. This is no new experience of the saints. In the apostolic times there were two classes of opposers against whom Christianity had to make its way, — the Jews and the Gentiles. The one of these required "a sign," while the others "sought after wisdom." The former would apply to the new faith a miraculous test, while the latter must needs see in it an infallible philosophy. Neither demand was without reason; and neither failed, in reality, to be met. Yet neither the miracle nor the philosophy was the chief attraction or principal value of the gospel, but rather its adaptation to the spiritual wants of mankind. Hence both the miracle-askers and the philosophy-seekers were liable to be disappointed, not coming to the investigation with spiritual hunger, but with a mere natural curiosity. But God does not put himself under examination by that spirit; and still less does he submit to tests fore-appointed by mere cavillers, — counting it unworthy of man's higher nature, and of the reverence due to himself. So "the wise and prudent" often, yea, generally, missed the right conclusion, and turned with contempt from the religion of the Nazarene; while in the very age of miracles, and when they were natural incidents of the gospel as a divine power, the sign-worshipping Jew not seldom asked in vain for the heaven-sent proof. "An evil and adulterous generation seeketh after a sign."

It is remarkable how history repeats itself in spiritual respects as well as otherwise. The unbelief of the human heart expresses itself now as of old. It has the same difficulties : it offers the same objections : it makes the same proposals. Every new sceptical volume, every additional article in a rationalistic periodical, illustrates this assertion: only it will be noticed that our modern doubters are not content with rejecting the gospel of Christ, but must needs take ground that shall make men hopeless of any gospel. They undermine the foundations even of natural religion, and cut men off from all direct approach to God. This appears in the antipathy which they show towards prayer, and in the pains which they ceaselessly take to prove that it is unphilosophical and absurd.

The famous anonymous letter (the authorship of which was afterwards acknowledged by Sir Henry Thompson, M.D.), communicated with a favorable note by Prof. Tyndall to "The Contemporary Review," suggested that it was time to put the question about prayer to a practical test, as would be done in the case of a disputed principle in natural science. The writer thus stated the case: "I ask that one single ward or hospital, under the care of first-rate physicians and surgeons, containing certain numbers of patients afflicted with those diseases which have been best studied, and of which the mortality rates are best known, whether the diseases are those which are treated by medical or by surgical remedies, should be, during a period of not less, say, than three or five years, made the object of special prayer by the whole body of the faithful ; and that, at the end of that time, the mortality rates should be compared with the past rates, and also with that of other leading hospitals similarly well managed, during the same period. Granting that time is given, and numbers are sufficiently large, so as to insure a minimum of error from accidental disturbing causes, the experiment will be exhaustive and complete."

To a superficial thinker such a test would easily appear to be reasonable ; and it might be claimed that the institution in Germany known as the Prayer Cure really meets it ; for that brings forward much proof of the power of prayer to effect the healing of disease, indirectly if not directly. And there is reason for the display of the power in that case ; since the institution proposes no object to aimless curiosity, or to cavilling scepticism, but is maintained on truly spiritual principles, — the prayer for healing being always carefully associated with efforts for the moral health of the afflicted. The grand difficulty with the proposed test is, that it wholly misses the true idea and philosophy of prayer, as set forth in the Bible. Sceptical scientists make sorry work when they undertake to reason about religion. They do not apprehend the first principles of a moral as distinguished from a material system. They partially understand nature, but have no right conception of the super-nature. God's moral universe has its peculiar adaptations of cause and effect, suited to its high spiritual ends. Prayer is a divine institution for human training on the side of character and not of mere science. It is related to divine providence, and not to natural causes. That providence is ordered with entire reference to the education of the human race in love, faith, humility, reverence, and obedience, and is made to hinge largely on prayer, or the application of individuals and communities to God for aid. The idea is not that prayer enlightens God as to the fact, or as to the supply of human wants ; or that it persuades him to change his mind, at man's entreaty : but prayer is a wise condition for God to annex to benefits which he is already inclined to bestow, in order that when given they may be attended with the best results. For spiritual ends it is often better that a thing should not be given, than that it should be given to a state of mind different from that which is secured by prayer, and by prayer alone. For God's great object is, to draw the soul as much as possible into a felt connection with himself in all things; that by a perpetual faith it may consciously live and rejoice in him. This spirit, essential to the good of the soul, is also essential to acceptance with God; for, as is said by the writer of the Epistle to the Hebrews, "He that cometh to God must believe that he is, and that he is the rewarder of them that diligently seek him." As prayer is the chief means of seeking

God, it may thus be understood that the two fundamental principles of religion are faith in God's existence, and faith in the efficacy of prayer. It is difficult to believe that any soul can fail of the spirit and results of religion, which truly prays. Many a sceptic has been reclaimed, when every other strand of faith had broken but a belief that God would hear prayer, and would guide the soul in the search after truth.

But it is evident, on a moment's thought, that to make prayer a bare application in words, irrespective of spirit, or to tender it to man unconditionally, as a power in nature, to be subject only to his will, like steam, or electricity, or gravity, would be to defeat its prime object. Yet the test proposed to be used in a hospital goes upon the idea, that

Christians claim that prayer involves a promise on the part of God to do every thing which men may ask; a pledge to place his omnipotence at their disposal. It needs not the mind of a philosopher to see that such a pledge would be a curse, and not a blessing. Power is a benefit, only as it is guided by wisdom; and until Christians become omniscient, God could not, with safety to the interests involved, bind himself to do whatever they should ask in prayer. Hence he requires prayer to be offered with humility and submission to the divine will, taking, as an example, the prayer of Jesus in the garden: "Nevertheless, not as I wilt, but as thou wilt." As death has not ceased to be the universal human doom, it would be folly to claim that the sick will always be healed in answer to prayer, so that the patients of a hospital-ward may be all cured, provided a prayer-meeting be held. Moreover, to propound such a test in a sceptical spirit, as does the writer of the letter, is at variance with the requirements of the Bible as to faith, and is only paralleled by the demand of the mocking Jews, when the Saviour hung upon the cross: "If he be the King of Israel, let him now come down from the cross, and we will believe him." In vain will the philosophers seek to wrest from us our chief weapon, leaving us defenceless amid the dangers of life. We know its value too well, to be thus despoiled.

> "Restraining prayer we cease to fight;
> Prayer makes the Christian's armoi bright;
> And Satan trembles when he sees
> The weakest saint upon his knees."

CHAPTER XV.

THE WEAPON TWO-EDGED.

IF prayer be a legitimate weapon to use against the enemies of our souls, the question arises, May it be used in a physical as well as a spiritual direction? Is the sword two-edged? Let us see.

The letter of a friend, which Prof. Tyndall gave to the public with commendation, proposing a hospital test for prayer, called forth such a protest from the Christian world, that he felt the necessity of explaining his views. This he did in a communication to "The Contemporary Review," entitled "Science and Religion," in which he resented the vituperative assaults of some of his theological critics, and asserted his own faith in prayer within certain limitations. He seems to believe in it as a natural instinct of men conscious of need, as having a happy influence on the mind, and as finding a possible sphere in the spiritual realm ; but he denies any room to its operation within the physical universe, which is controlled by unchanging laws with which God will not interfere. He does not deny that God could interpose in the physical realm, so far as his power is concerned ; but he affirms that there is no reason to believe that God does so interpose, or that his world-plan admits of such an act. The theory of prayer has no proof. Hence no one should pray for any result of a physical nature. His position will be plain from the following citations : —

"The bone of contention at present is *the physical value of prayer*. . . . Physical nature is not its legitimate domain. This conclusion, moreover, must be based on pure physical evidence, and not on any inherent unreasonableness in the act of prayer. The theory that the system of nature is under the control of a Being who changes phenomena in compliance with the prayers of men, is, in my opinion, a perfectly legitimate one. . . . It is matter of experience that an earthly father, who is at the same time both wise and tender, listens to the requests of his children, and, if they do not ask amiss, takes pleasure in granting their requests. We know also that this compliance extends to the alteration, within certain limits, of the current events of earth. With this suggestion offered by our experience, it is no departure from scientific method, to place behind natural phenomena a universal Father, who, in answer to the prayers of his children, alters the currents of those phenomena. Thus far Theology and Science go hand in hand. . . . But without *verification* a theoretic conception is a mere figment of the intellect; and I am sorry to find us parting company at this point. . . . Often unreasonable if not contemptible, in its purer forms prayer hints at disciplines which few of us can neglect without moral loss. But no good can come of giving it a delusive value, by claiming for it a power in physical nature. It may strengthen the heart to meet life's losses, and thus indirectly promote physical well-being."

Now, as human reason is the grand test with the anti-prayer philosophers, let us see if the position here assumed stands to reason. Prayer is admitted to be a natural instinct of a dependent creature like man. He is in need ; and prayer to God, the spontaneous utterance of his felt wants, is as natural and inevitable as any other instinctive act, — as the appeal of the young of any animal to the parent, or of human children to their fathers and mothers. Now, will Prof. Tyndall tell us of any instance in God's creation, in which an instinct is implanted, for which there is no provision in the world without? The newborn child has an instinctive desire of milk ; and behold, the mother's breast furnishes the supply. Every instinct points to an outward fact. This is as sure as any thing taught by science. It is one of the facts of science. But if that be true, then the instinct of prayer in the human soul indicates infallibly a provision in the divine arrangements to meet it, — a provision which is as truly part of the system of things undei which we live as is the law of gravity. Man prays, because over against this instinctive utterance of his sense of need stands the fact of a prayer-hearing heavenly Father. We claim this upon scientific grounds, as the teaching of nature itself.

But does this instinct limit itself to one class of wants? Are men never instinctively prompted to pray for physical relief? Does the sick man offer no petition for restoration to health? Does the mother beseech no divine pity, when her child is threatened with death? Does the shipwrecked sailor utter no cry to God? Have stricken communities no ground for an appeal to the Father above, when drought, famine, pestilence, or other physical calamity, impends, or perhaps already crushes? Surely the instinct may be said to be strong and universal in precisely such cases, as the whole history of mankind attests. The soul would despair, the man would often die, could one not pray for relief in physical distress. But, if we may rightfully and must necessarily pray, then there is a provision in God's scheme for an answer within the physical realm.

It does not suffice to say that prayer, although not obtaining the thing sought, aids the soul by its incidental influence; by lifting it into communion with God, and filling it with noble and pure thoughts. It cannot do even this except as the soul believes in its efficacy as petition; for the moment a man ceases to think that prayer will avail to obtain the needed blessing, and is convinced by the philosophers that it is only a meditation which re-acts upon the mind for its spiritual good, he will no longer continue the vain form of petition for divine aid. And what a curious instinct that would be, which should prompt to an act which has no direct meaning and use, but is only incidentally of value! As if a babe should have an instinct for milk, not to receive milk from the mother's breast, but only to nestle by her side, and be warmed by her body! or, as if the instinct for milk was only to enable the child to comfort itself by the presence and feeling of the mother, while it died from the lack of milk !

But why should Prof. Tyndall place this limitation on prayer? What is there in the physical universe which makes prayer inapplicable to it, while the spiritual realm is open to its influence? He will reply, perhaps, that the physical universe has fixed laws, in accordance with which its events occur. That is true ; but the same may be affirmed of the spiritual universe. It also has fixed laws, appropriate to the nature of mind ; and in accordance with those mental laws events take place. If divine laws rule prayer out of the material world, there can be no place for it in the spiritual world. Yea, as the spiritual realm is the higher of the two, its laws may be properly conceived of as more inviolable than those of physics, and as, therefore, a greater obstacle to prayer. Prof. Tyndall's philosophy reverses the order of reason. When one thinks of the mystery of thought, of feeling, and of will, and of the difficulty of harmonizing divine action with creature-freedom, it is much easier to conceive of prayer as being answered in reference to physical than to spiritual results. It must be easier to operate in the lower than in the higher realm. Prof. Tyndall's distinction operates against him; and his limitation (if one be valid at all) is quite misplaced. Indeed, from some of his language we doubt whether he would affirm that prayer brings any direct answer from God even in the spiritual realm; though *at present* he only discusses its physical relations.

But the supposed necessity for the limitation arises from a misconception of the relation of prayer to divine law. Prayer being as much provided for in the divine system as is gravity, electricity, heat, or light in physics, or as are thought, feeling, and will in the spirit realm, we may be sure that it is not out of harmony with the other forces. There is no need of supposing that when prayer operates in either realm, there is any setting-aside of the laws of the realm. There is simply a new use, combination, and direction of them by the unseen divine will, analogous to the effects constantly wrought by the human will in both of these same realms. Take a simple illustration. A child asks his father to do a certain thing. His father consents; and the child goes away satisfied. In doing it, the father produces, in answer to his child's request, results that otherwise would not have occurred. Those results grow out of the direct use of some of nature's laws, the counteraction of others, and the combination of others. We will suppose that chestnuts were to be gathered and boiled. To do this the father counteracts the law of gravity by bringing his own body into action, by throwing sticks into the tree, and by picking up and bringing in the chestnuts. He uses that law in causing the nuts to fall from the tree to the ground. He combines the operation of various chemical laws, as he kindles a fire, heats the water, and boils the nuts to softness. When the boy returns, he finds that his prayer has been answered in a way unseen by himself, and within the physical realm. Now, why cannot God as truly and as easily answer prayer in the realm of physics, in a way unseen by us, and without suspension or violation of the laws of nature? We pray for the recovery of a sick friend. No miracle is needed in order to secure an answer, unless it be a case in which organic destruction has already occurred, as when the lungs have been consumed. In such a case God has already indicated his will; and prayer is inappropriate. The result may come by a wise use of a natural law, which God shall secure in answer to the prayer. He may act directly on vital forces; or he may so influence the minds of friends as to draw attention to the proper remedy or to the most skilful physician or to the most faithful nurse. Shall we deny so credible a fact, because we do not know precisely how God may influence human thought? That were to elevate ignorance into a demonstration. Reason and faith agree that the Creator may employ his own laws in answer to the prayers of his children. He is not less able, in this respect, than an earthly parent, but infinitely more able. We may thus see that no argument from Scripture is needed against Prof. Tyndall's view. Philosophy, science, and common sense are sufficient to refute him. He can neither wrest from faith its chief weapon, nor blunt either of its edges.

> " Then, my soul, in every strait
> To thy Father come, and wait;
> He will answer every prayer:
> God is present everywhere."

CHAPTER XVI.

THE WEAPON TESTED.

PROF. TYNDALL, in his second communication to the "Contemporary Review" on prayer, admitted the idea of prayer to God, as our heavenly Father, to be an excellent theory, could it only be proved to be true, as one verifies a theory of light or of heat, by experiments addressed to the outward senses. He complained that Christian people object to all physical tests of prayer, such as the famous proposition to test its power in a particular ward of a hospital; and yet he knew no other method of settling the dispute. Indeed, he thought that the physical test settles it against the Christian. Let us reflect a little upon this idea of verifying prayer.

If prayer be a real power, as a petition to God for the production of desired effects in the spiritual and in the physical world, then the fact must be capable of verification. It would be unwise to recommend and even to enjoin its use as a weapon in our spiritual warfare, were there no way in which to test its edge and temper. The promises and invitations of Scripture imply that there is a way. God invites us to pray, and pledges an appropriate answer. But it does not follow that the process of verification is in all respects the same as in the case of a mere physical law. The principle, however, will be the same; which is, that when the prescribed conditions are fulfilled the promised effect will be produced. Thus gunpowder will not explode unless it be dry. Not a few of Prof. Tyndall's admirable experiments in illustration of physical law would fail, if one or two seemingly slight conditions were neglected by himself or his assistant. So it is in prayer; only the conditions are moral. God promises to hear the prayer of the humble, penitent, obedient, believing, importunate, persevering, yet submissive soul, which asks for a true good, according to the divine mind. If the conditions are not fulfilled (and it is largely to secure their presence that prayer is prescribed), the answer must not be expected. But these conditions are not visible to the eye, are not to be detected by any outward sense, and only God perfectly knows whether they are complied with. How is it possible, then, to test prayer in a mere outward mechanical way, by setting people to praying for a specific outward result without reference to the spiritual relations of the matter, which are vital to the process? Water-power or steam-power can be turned on machinery at will, merely by moving a lever that connects or disconnects the power; but prayer-power cannot be so ordered, in the very nature of the case. Who shall previously guarantee that the object sought is, in the divine view, the best to be granted? Who shall certify those who witness the so-called experiment, that those who pray ask in a penitent and obedient state of mind, or with fervor and importunity, or with mingled faith and submission? Yet the law of prayer is suspended on these conditions of moral force as really as Prof. Tyndall knows the manifestations of heat to be on some exertion of physical force. Why, then, should he ask that the moral question of answers to prayer be treated as a mere physical problem?

And here it should be noted, that as prayer is an exercise within the spiritual realm, having its reasons in moral ends, though often producing effects in the physical world, and as it demands peculiar spiritual conditions, so it will never afford evidence of its reality by a demonstration which shall compel belief in an unsympathetic and sceptical mind. Nothing is mathematically demonstrated in religion ; and, in truth, very little is so demonstrated in science. High probability, amounting to a reasonable certainty, on which one may confidently act, is all that either religion or physical science logically offers. What are called universal physical laws are accepted from faith in the uniformity of natural causes, and are probable inferences from observed phenomena, scarcely one of which might not suddenly fail : that is, no one absolutely knows that an exceptional phenomenon may not be discovered tomorrow ; as the seemingly universal law that bodies expand with heat and contract with cold, finds an exception in water, which obeys the law till the freezing-point is reached, and then reverses it. Still more must religion have its laws accepted from faith in the uniform operation of God as an intelligent being at the head of a moral government ; who will always act on the same principles of righteousness and benevolence, and who will necessarily subordinate the lower physical realm to the higher spiritual realm. But nothing in the spiritual realm evidences itself to a gross, materialistic, sceptical mind. Not even God himself appears to be a reality; and the atheistic philosopher complains that he can obtain no tangible evidence that God exists and acts. He uses Tyndall's very argument, saying, that the idea of God is a very pretty theory, in itself not without attraction and a certain analogy with human experiences; but unfortunately it is not capable of being verified in the physical world. Nobody produces God to him; nobody shows him phenomena which he can attribute to no other than a directly divine origin. How, then, is the reality of prayer to verify itself to such a state of mind? Let the subsequent phenomena be what they might, they would be explained away on some other supposition, as were the miracles of Jesus by the unbelieving Jews, who witnessed them. And Jesus truly said of the unsympathetic, sceptical class, "Neither would they believe though one rose from the dead." It is no part of religion to *compel* belief: its aim is to mould character, and therefore it simply *invites* belief on evidence credible to a candid mind. Those who have faith in God as at the head of a moral government over dependent yet responsible creatures, will have faith in prayer. The same kind of evidence establishes both facts.

Furthermore, it is worthy of Mr. Tyndall's reflection that those who have made the largest trial of prayer are the best satisfied of its power. They have made the only experiments that the nature of the case allows, — experiments not of mere scientific curiosity, or as a method of placating opposition or silencing sceptics, by which God shall submit himself to infidel testings; but experiments of personal petition for objects providentially pressed upon them, and in compliance with the spiritual conditions requisite. The church has always been a praying church; its prayers have extended to all manner of objects; and its experience has so confirmed its faith, that never did it pray more frequently or more fervently than to-day. This is very singular, if prayer is a failure as to the production of desired results. The Bible gives us, in its historical portions, numerous instances of prayer for specific events to take place, both in the physical and in the spiritual realm of things; and those events occurred. It may be easy for Prof. Tyndall to deny the fact (which does not at all disprove it), or to call the result in each case a mere coincidence. But these coincidences have been so many and so marked, in every generation, and in the case of every prayerful individual, that faith has found abundant evidence on which to live, and it is of no use for men who do not pray to seek to invalidate it. Those who make honest trial find success.

We may refer Prof. Tyndall to the recorded facts in connection with the means obtained by Francke through prayer, in special emergencies, to build the orphan house at Halle, and to the experience of George Müller at Bristol,

THE WEAPON TESTED. 171

in his own land. Or, as he especially desires to test prayer in connection with healing disease, we would ask him to read a little book called "Dorothea Trudel, or The Prayer of Faith," published in London, and republished also in this country; in which he will learn of facts which stood the test of a legal trial before an unsympathetic court in Zurich, Switzerland, which were confessed to be true by intelligent physicians, and which gained the credence, after careful examination, of such theologians as Tholuck and Bishop Kapff. We do not claim that it is possible to *show* the relation of prayer to the effect in a way of visible demonstration, as though it were a mechanical force to be illustrated by machinery, for such is not its nature; but we do claim that experience proves prayer to be precisely what it is described as being in the Holy Scriptures; that it is effective for the purposes, in the ways, and on the conditions there set forth.

> "The Saviour bids thee watch and pray,
>   Maintain a warrior's strife;
> O Christian! hear his voice to-day:
>   Obedience is thy life."

CHAPTER XVII.

VICTORY THROUGH SELF-DENIAL.

ONE cannot read the New Testament without being struck with the prominent place which it gives to self-denial. The words of Jesus might be taken as the motto for a Christian life, "If any man will come after me, let him deny himself, and take up his cross, and follow me." No conception of religion can be true in which self-indulgence is the law of life, or in which self-denial is nearly or quite ignored. There can be no victory in this lifelong war, unless we give heed to the apostle, "Thou therefore endure hardness as a good soldier of Jesus Christ. No man that warreth entangleth himself with the affairs of life; that he may please him who hath chosen him to be a soldier."

Yet one will gain no genuine advantage from merely repeating the word "self-denial," as though there were some spiritual charm in it, or in cherishing a narrow conception of what the virtue means and implies. Suppose we look the matter squarely in the face.

Self-denial is used, and not altogether improperly, in various related but yet distinct senses. In its most comprehensive sense it includes all Christian character, as based on the principle of self-renunciation. As selfishness, or supreme self-love, is the essence of sin ; so self-denial, or the putting self down to its proper position, in subordination to God's glory and the common welfare, is the reversing and opposing principle of piety. This is the principal idea in the words of Jesus quoted above, — that one cannot be his disciple without denying that ruling self-love which has previously constituted the aim of life, and substituting for it the love of God and the neighbor.

From this general principle result specific acts in which, out of love to Christ, a disciple denies himself a gratification which appeals to natural desire in a way of sin. He will not seek pleasure by evil methods, among vile associates, by dangerous courses, or at improper times. The pleasure itself would often be strongly attractive, were it separated from sin in its circumstances ; but he denies himself gratification in that direction, not being willing to do wrong and

to grieve his Saviour. But, more than
this: the disciple who is imbued with
the spirit of the Master will also often
deny himself innocent gratifications,
when by so doing he can better promote the cause of Christ, and the good
of his fellow-men. Christ's own life
was, in this sense, a continuous act of
self-denial. He submitted to the humiliation of an earthly career and a
human experience; he made hourly sacrifice of personal ease and comfort, to
benefit the bodies and souls of men;
and he exposed himself to the bitter assaults and finally to the murderous attack of those who hated the truth which
he proclaimed, and the purity which he
exemplified. Well did Paul set forth
this duty of love, when, affirming that
we "ought not to please ourselves," he

added, "Let every one of us please his neighbor for his good unto edification; for even Christ pleased not himself," etc. In other words, the spirit of love is self-sacrificing: it will joyfully yield a personal gratification to benefit or please the loved object. Life is full of this self-denial in natural directions; as in the toils and sufferings which parents undergo for children, and children too, oftentimes, for parents. Religion leads us to act similarly for the good of any one who is in need of our help. Thus our lives may be daily and almost hourly occupied with greater and smaller sacrifices of innocent personal pleasure, made in behalf of others. Loving sacrifice is a Christly law, which we prescribe to ourselves. This law it is always healthful to expound and illustrate.

We must recommend it to others, and must live it out ourselves. If God is love, if Christ was love, if love is the fulfilling of the law, then self-denial is an inevitable accompaniment of a holy life.

But to believe this, and to act continually upon it, is in no wise inconsistent with our taking a great deal of pleasure in life, both in work and play, in society and in amusement. For a little reflection shows that the highest good of all concerned is best promoted by this very course, and that asceticism, on a large or on a small scale, is no proper form of self-denial. It is a mistaken and often an injurious practice, conveying wrong ideas of a religious life, and not seldom resulting in a narrow, self-righteous censoriousness in those who conform to it, and in a confirmed dislike of piety on the part of those whom they drive into antagonism. Much better is it to partake of all innocent delight in life, thereby helping the happiness of those with whom we associate, and preserving a natural character to piety, while yet we count no gratification too dear to be set aside at any moment, in order to promote a greater good. Many a Christian father would have more of the spirit of true love, and would have more religious influence over his children, if he would often (self-denyingly, if necessary) unbend from serious studies and grave labors, and join merrily in their diversions. Some would call this a pleasure ; but if to others it is a self-denial, then let them practise that virtue. And so of other social gratifications which make life more pleasant and none the less holy.

But it is a sad fact that Christian teachers sometimes harp upon self-denial as if it were a something separate from the spontaneous sacrifice of a loving spirit, to be every hour manifested in a hundred little thoughtful ways of mutual helpfulness, and to be occasionally exemplified more severely upon providential occasions. They talk and write as if it were the doing of a certain class of unpleasant acts, or the refusing to enjoy certain specified pleasures; as if, in the sight of our loving Father, there were any merit in an unnecessary deprivation, — an idea born of ancient Phariseeism, and adopted and put to large service by modern Romanism. The truth is, we are apt to run in ruts of our own, made for the wheels o. thought by our temperament, education, and peculiar experience. And so we have pet self-denials, to which we would fain make fellow-saints conform. When we speak of the virtue of self-denial we have our eye upon particular methods ; which, indeed, may be those to which we are called, but which we are not therefore warranted in imposing on others, charging our brethren with not practising self-denial, if, perchance, they do not accept them at our hands. God may see that, in other ways, equally appropriate to their circumstances, they are gladly making many and great sacrifices for his loved cause. No man in the Christian realm has a patent of self-denial, that others should be compelled to come to him to find the best method.

A heart full of love will need little prompting in this direction, and will fall back on no stereotyped rules for ordering the details of life, so as to manifest the spirit of self-sacrifice. As tears of joy and of sorrow come from the same fountain, so it often happens that the same good man runs over with humor and with tender sympathy; is the life of a feast, and the chief comforter in the house of mourning; enters into innocent pleasures with peculiar zest, and sacrifices them without a struggle when thereby he can do good to the bodies or souls of others. There is meaning, in this respect as well as in others, in the familiar lines, —

> "If on our daily course our mind
> Be set, to hallow all we find,
> New treasures still, of countless price,
> God will provide for sacrifice.

The trivial round, the common task,
Will furnish all we ought to ask, —
Room to deny ourselves ; a road
To bring us daily nearer God."

CHAPTER XVIII.

VICTORY THROUGH SORROW.

THAT a holy life should be joyous, is what reason would expect, and is what religion affirms. For does it not imply the testimony of a good conscience, which is itself positive bliss? Is it not also a restful faith in God, which is the essence of peace? Does it not, as being love, carry with it a benevolent gratification in all the happiness and the holiness of others? And must it not involve a sense of Divine approbation and favor, which is the summit of joy?

But how as to its external experience? Will all outward circumstances be so arranged by divine Providence as to conduce to immediate pleasure? This might, at first, be supposed to be so; for the conformity of the outward to the inward is a natural idea. The body is the expression and complement of the soul. The material universe is in wondrous analogy, throughout, with the intellectual and moral. Holiness, moreover, has the promise of bliss in all forms, as a fitting reward. God, too, as a benevolent being, must delight in bestowing gifts. How, then, could it be possible, it might be asked, for God to order it otherwise than that holiness should invariably be associated with blissful external experiences?

Facts show that this is not the case; and sound reason joins with inspired Scripture to tell us why. Strong, pure, incorruptible character could not thus be formed. Character must be a growth from small beginnings, and in the face of temptation. The soul must be put on trial; and that necessitates an arrangement which shall make holiness cost somewhat. All probation involves this element,— a temporary and partial sacrifice of personal happiness, in order to sustain the law which honors God and protects the universal good. Some form of gratification must be foregone, to abide the test which God has appointed. One's own ease or pleasure must, to some extent, be laid aside, in order to preserve or aid or rescue others. Self-denial becomes thus a leading virtue, in a state of probation. Native instincts are restrained within prescribed bounds, as a proof of obedience;

or are denied as a means of promoting the happiness of others, and thus as a fulfilment of the golden law of love. Doubtless some such self-denying test was set before the angels in their probationary condition; and Satan refused compliance, and was followed in his evil example by a multitude of his associates. Adam and Eve came under the same probationary law; and, tempted by a natural desire to eat of inviting fruit and to gain attractive knowledge,—a gratification which they were unwilling to forego to please God,—they violated the divine command, and fell from holy character.

If this restriction on pleasure is needful prior to a fall, how much more must it hold true in a redemptive scheme, which aims to restore sinners to holiness!

They have become selfish; and the object is, to render them benevolent,—to induce in them a character of love which shall set the welfare of others above personal gratification, and shall be true to God at the cost of self-denial. They have become unbelieving; and the object is, to renew in them a firm faith in God, such as shall trust him in despite of the most unfavorable appearances, and even in the face of personal suffering.

Thus it is that men find the world to be full of sorrow, it being also full of sin. The way out of the sin is usually through the sorrow; as multitudes have found to their subsequent exceeding joy. The Israelites fought hard to gain the land of Canaan in exchange for their desert-life. The way to rest led not only through the Jordan, but through many a bloody battle. Victory comes to all as the consequence and reward of suffering. This is not because God delights in the sorrow, as though it were a good in itself; but because he is wise enough to see its value and necessity as a means, and is sufficiently firm and intelligent in his benevolence, to use it for the ultimate good of men.

Take those whose unbelief fails to recognize God in daily providence, or to have regard to his government, and whose selfishness perverts his continual bounty into occasion of deeper sin; and how shall there begin to be made on them an impression of the reality of God's being and agency, and of his holy character, save by some interruption of their pleasures? God must needs awe and startle them into a reception of the primary truths of religion. In this way many a man has lost his fortune, and saved his soul; has seen his vessel go upon the rocks, but has escaped spiritual shipwreck; has stood aghast while his idols were shattered in pieces, but has received God afterward as his eternal portion. Some states of atmosphere can only be purified by raging storms, which, in their destructiveness, threaten to bring back chaos again. In such a case love sends the storm, and even smiles amid the desolation.

Nor can the triumph of good over evil in the redeemed soul after conversion proceed to perfection, without the steady discipline of sorrow. Hence we notice that some of the best men on earth have been the most afflicted also.

It was Job, "perfect and upright," a man "that feared God, and eschewed evil," whose misfortunes became proverbial. All history resounds with the plaints of sufferers who could not understand why they should be crushed to the earth with trouble, while the wicked rioted in prosperity. The Psalmist explained, that, in his own case, his sorrows were appointed with divine faithfulness, not as destroying judgments, but as means of grace, to release him from sin: "Before I was afflicted I went astray; but now have I kept Thy word." And what saint has not had a similar experience? Therefore the New Testament assures us that God "scourgeth every son whom he receiveth," and that to be without chastisement is to be a bastard.

It is no small mistake, then, to think

that trouble and misfortune operate only adversely; that they simply discourage and depress men; that they fill the mind with undue anxiety, and make it grovel amid earthly and sensual thoughts; that they harden and imbitter the soul against both God and man. Such an effect does, indeed, often ensue; but it is due not to the trouble, but to absence of faith in God. Woe, indeed, to the man who fails to cling to God in the time of his trial! He may go insane in the hour of his sudden calamity, as did not a few rich men from the effect of the Chicago fire; but as did not Job, in his far sorer misfortunes, who could say, "Though He slay me, yet will I trust in him." When faith is present, a moral victory is won over the fierce and Satanic temptation to distrust and despair.

Patience and fortitude bear up under the present pain, while hope of future and everlasting good creates a smile upon the very face of sorrow. Yea, sometimes such is the spiritual victory, that the soul, amid the sorest pressure of earthly trial, cries aloud in holy exultation, "These light afflictions, which are but for a moment, work for us a far more exceeding and eternal weight of glory." Thus comes true the inspired word, "No chastening for the present seemeth to be joyous, but grievous: nevertheless, afterward it yieldeth the peaceable fruit of righteousness unto them who are exercised thereby."

We do well, then, to feel that there is something sacred in sorrow ; that, though God's goodness prompts him to bestow gifts immediately pleasant in their reception, yet he is never more near to the soul, or more tender of it, than when it is in deepest waters of affliction. It is said that fruits ripen in the sunshine; and yet half of each twenty-four hours God puts the vegetable world into darkness, to say nothing of the clouds and storms which so often intercept the rays of the sun during the day. Character ripens under afflictions as well as under enjoyments. Sorrow refines the selfishness and the earthliness out of the soul, cools the fever of its sinful ambition, turns its face upward and Godward, teaches it to lead a life of faith, and brings it off victor in the deadly conflict.

> "Blest is the hope that holds to God
>   In doubt and darkness still unshaken,
>   And sings along the heavenly road,
>   Sweetest, when most it seems forsaken."

CHAPTER XIX.

VICTORY THROUGH JOY.

NATURE and grace alike testify that there is strength in joy. It is no uncommon matter of observation, that a sorrowful man is a dispirited man. Melancholy breeds despair. Tears in the eyes blind the sight. Even when sanctified affliction imparts new power to the soul, as unquestionably it does, so that there is a victory through sorrow, it is by an exercise of faith which supplants the natural grief by a joy and peace in God, — a truth recognized by the words of Scripture concerning "chastening," that "*afterward* it worketh the *peaceable* fruit of righteousness."

Soldiers fight best when well fed and well sheltered, and when confidence in their cause, in their officers, in their numbers, and in their discipline gives a joyful assurance of success.

That was a noteworthy remark of Nehemiah, when he bade the people go to their homes for feasting instead of weeping, saying, "Neither be ye sorry; for the joy of the Lord is your strength." So, when the Psalmist has described the people of God as full of gladness, and as constantly engaged in praise, he adds, "They go from strength to strength." And does not Paul intimate a similar connection of experiences, when he writes to the Corinthians, "We are helpers of your joy, for by faith ye stand;" and when he prayed for the Colossians, that they "might be strengthened with all might, according to his glorious power, unto all patience and long-suffering with joyfulness"?

A mere natural joy, such as flows from the possession of natural good, — health, friends, riches, food, society, — may be, indeed, a temptation and an occasion of defeat rather than of victory. The soul may rest in such good as its portion, and may thus separate from God. It was not enough to preserve our first parents in holiness, that they dwelt in Paradise, where all their surroundings were pleasant. They did not lack a supply for a single want, nor had they the least anxiety for the future. They had had no bitter experiences, and nothing had occurred to associate piety with gloom. Yet, amid all manner of natural joys, they lost their faith in God, under a false suggestion of the tempter, and not even gratitude, — that easiest of virtues, — held them to their allegiance.

If this were so with unfallen natures, much more must there be danger that men in their depravity will forget God, in the midst of outward prosperity. It was written of Jeshurun, that he "waxed fat and kicked." The rich man, of whom Jesus spake in the parable, was " clothed in purple and fine linen, and fared sumptuously every day;" but that fact produced no tendency to piety in heart or life. Similarly, " the rich fool," of another parable, was only led by his increase of goods to say to his soul, " Eat, drink, and be merry." The rich are far from being the pious class of society; natural as it would seem for abounding blessings to produce abounding thanks. Indeed, our Saviour reproved and warned them as he never did the poor, and declared that it was with difficulty that any of them could be saved !

Yet there is a triumph of grace on the joyful side of human experience. Although God ordinarily needs to afflict us much, as we pass through the world, in order that we may be weaned from mere natural good, may take refuge in him alone, and may be trained in self-denial, yet one of the evidences of sanctification is, the ability to rejoice in all the pleasant things of this life without being ensnared by them. If grace did not often accomplish this result, it would appear deficient in power, and not suitably related to the necessities of human life. Piety would be associated with gloom, and poverty would be the only and the narrow sphere of religion. But the saints also illustrate godliness amid prosperous scenes. Nicodemus and Joseph of Arimathea appear among the believers in Jesus, as well as the poor fishermen of Galilee. And surely it must be a delight to God to find a sanctified soul whom it is safe to bless with a large degree of earthly good; for giving rather than withholding is his habitual act, as love is his very nature. Towards this condition He must be training all his people. For what is our conception of heaven but of a place and state in which God eternally links together purity and joy, because each is there promotive of the other? In proportion, then, as one ripens for heaven, will he not come into the state in which he will be able to enjoy all manner of good, and to be united only the more closely to God by his pleasant surroundings? What a victory that is over man's selfish and godless character, which naturally uses earthly enjoyment as a substitute for God, loving the gift but not the Giver!

And surely, among the triumphs of grace in this world, is yet to be a prevailing piety which shall make all the benefits of civilization tributary to itself; so that the Christianized multitudes shall not dwell in the hovels of poverty, but shall joyfully shout, "The lines are fallen unto us in pleasant places, and we have a goodly heritage!" It is a foretokening of this result, when we see individual Christians blessed with worldly comfort, yet not made thereby worldly in spirit, but rather refined and elevated in character, and filled with holy gratitude and love. There are those, — few, as yet, it must be confessed, — to whom all outward joys are wings that bear them Godward. As wealth increases, their liberality keeps equal pace, and they find the more occasion for honoring God and for blessing their fellow-men. Such is their spirit of consecration, that they never separate between God and providential mercies, but enjoy both together. The more they have, the more they love. The more they enjoy, the closer God seems to be to them. That which to others is a fatal temptation is to them a means of grace. What is such an experience but a foretaste of heaven, and a restoration of the soul and its surroundings to their truly natural condition? Thus a beginning is made of that state in which "God shall wipe away all tears from their eyes, and there shall be no more death, neither sorrow, nor crying, neither shall there be any more pain;" in which, as God multiplies his blessings, the grateful and joyous soul triumphs more and more, in the increase of knowledge and power, and in the ecstacy of love.

> "Rejoice in God alway;
> When earth looks heavenly bright,
> When joy makes glad the livelong day,
> And peace shuts in the night."

CHAPTER XX.

VICTORY AT THE OUTPOSTS.

NOT a small part of spiritual, as of military success, depends on the care taken of the outposts. These may easily be undervalued. They have none of the magnificence of a grand camp about them. Each is occupied by a few soldiers at most, and often by only a single sentinel. It may seem to be a very trifling business, to do nothing but to watch, and to send an occasional report to headquarters. The glory of war is associated with the thunder of great guns, the sharp rattle of musketry, the ringing sound of the trumpet, the drawing-up in battle-array of armies, the waving of banners, the rush of cavalry, the deadly assault, the smoke of conflict, the huzza of victory. How unlike all this is the still life, the solitary employment, at a distant outpost! There is no romance in mere vigilance. Passion is stirred by attack. One feels that he is part of a host, and himself an element of power, when marching in the ranks of the main army, or abiding in the tented field; but there is little to stir enthusiasm in being sent away into the woods, or to distant hills, to watch for what may never appear, to guard what may never be attacked. As though the enemy would trouble himself about insignificant outposts, when there is a central camp to be assaulted!

Yet who does not know that danger begins at the outposts? These must be passed before the camp can be reached; and, if the enemy meditates a surprise, nothing can prevent it but the vigilance of the distant sentinels. They have the honor and responsibility of being nearest the foe. Many an army has been lost by the neglect of the commander to take sufficient precautions against a sudden night attack. Many a castle and city has been captured through the absence of even a single sentinel from his beat. The rules of war are severe on this point. It will not do to allow one man to endanger an army; and so death has often been the fate of a guard found asleep on his post.

These facts have their counterpart in the spiritual conflict. There are outposts of the soul, where danger usually begins, where the enemy first shows himself, and where consequently vigilance must be perpetual. Here comes an application of the old Latin maxim: *Obsta principiis:* "Resist the beginnings of evil." Do not let the enemy effect a lodgement any where. Allow him not to pass the outposts. Be prepared for the small temptations. Watch the doubtful points. Investigate the suspicious movements. Remember that the foe comes often in disguise; that Satan appears as "an angel of light;" that sin calls itself pleasure, and never proclaims its own guilt. "Watch and pray" is the order issued from headquarters. A step at a time is all that our adversary cares to be allowed to take; and usually he can take all he desires, one after another, if he is allowed the first.

The chief outposts are the senses.

Bunyan, in his allegory of "Mansoul," well called them the gates of the city, and described what was done at Eargate, Eye-gate, &c.. But how few think it important to guard the senses lest they be the inlets of temptation! So far, indeed, are many from guarding them, that they throw the gates wide open, that there may enter what will! Curiosity is so powerful in some minds, and the love of novelty and excitement in others, that they place no restraint on eye or ear or mouth or nostril or hand. They determine to know all that is going on, to see whatever is to be seen, to hear whatever is to be heard. That this takes them needlessly into the midst of temptation, to places which they should shun as dangerous, to sights which pollute the mind, to sounds which enervate the soul, to company which solicits to evil, they do not seem to weigh. And yet the history of sin at every point suggests a caution in this very respect, showing how even the strongest have fallen by allowing the enemy to capture this outpost of the senses. Let us notice a few facts.

How did Satan begin his first campaign on earth? He appealed to the outward senses: he drew Eve's attention to the beauty of the forbidden fruit, and to its attractiveness to the palate, thus enlisting the powerful appeal of the senses on his side. Her only course of safety was to leave the spot; to refuse longer to look at the tempting fruit. But this she did not: she allowed a strong desire to be aroused, which aided the lying declarations of the tempter, and the result was that she yielded. "She saw that the tree was good for food, and that it was pleasant to the eyes." And how came David's sad fall about? Simply by not guarding this same outpost of the eyes. He looked in a wrong direction, on an object of powerful temptation; he kept on looking, till his animal nature was inflamed, and a flood of passion carried his will along as mere driftwood. The world is not even yet through with the sad results of that neglect to watch one of the outward senses. Yet many who claim to be Christians will indulge that same sense in a not dissimilar way, in the ball-room, at the theatre, at the opera, and in other places where female charms are meretriciously displayed! Parents will sometimes allow their children to go and "look on," amid scenes in which they would not allow them actively to participate. What effect can this have but to inflame desire through the eye and ear, and to create in the children a taste for dissipating pleasures?

How forcible, in this view, is the declaration of Isaiah, that one of the characteristics of the man who "shall dwell on high," and shall be under special divine protection, is, that he "shutteth his eyes from seeing evil"! How instructive, for a similar reason, is the affirmation of Job, that he had "made a covenant with his eyes not to look upon a maid" in a way likely to prove a temptation to his virtue! How wise the direction of Solomon to the young man, when in the presence of moral danger; "Let thine eyes look right on, and let thine eyelids look straight before thee"! that is, do not pause to parley with temptation; do not give the temptation a chance to rouse your baser passions. The philosophy of human nature and the precepts of religion dictate this same course in the whole range of spiritual conflict. They expose the folly of leaving the senses unguarded; because evil presents its solicitations, the memory lodges within it vile associations, the imagination is polluted, and the way is prepared for overt sin. Inaugurate victory at the outposts.

> "I want a godly fear,
>   A quick, discerning eye,
>   That looks to see where sin is near,
>   And sees the tempter fly;
>   A spirit still prepared,
>   And armed with jealous care,
>   Forever standing on its guard,
>   And watching unto prayer."

CHAPTER XXI.

CONTINUAL VICTORY.

WHAT the soul needs is not occasional, but perpetual aid. Its wants never intermit, its enemies are always at hand, its temptations are omnipresent. The hour arrives not, nay, the moment never comes, when it can stand alone. Essential weakness is its own nature, separate from God. Its safety is in a wondrous capacity to be filled, inspired, and energized by God. To be thus divinely possessed and used is its true life and power. But that the life and power may be continuous, the divine indwelling must be perpetual.

Continual spiritual victory is then conditioned on abiding faith in Jesus as an ever-present Saviour, who is always "with" the universal church, the smallest Christian group, and the humblest individual, according to his several promises : "Lo, I am with you alway, even unto the end of the world." "Where two or three are gathered together in my name, there am I in the midst of them." "If a man love me, he will keep my words, and my Father will love him, and we will come unto him and make our abode with him." An occasional Christ, to come to our aid now and then in special emergencies, would not meet our spiritual necessities. It would be a limitation too much like that which attended the earthly mission of Jesus, "in the days of his flesh." When he was in Galilee, he was away from Jerusalem When he was healing the sick, or teaching the multitudes by the seaside, he could not minister similarly to human wants in the temple. And so he said to his disciples that it was "expedient" for him "to go away," that, by the presence and power of the Comforter, the Holy Spirit, he might be the more fully with them. Thus they would have a double conception of him: as "a great High Priest passed into the heavens," by reason of whose perpetual intercession they could "come boldly unto the throne of grace," and could "obtain mercy and find grace to help in time of need;" and as "Christ in them," a sanctifying presence, penetrating their whole being with the influences of the Spirit.

Now, this is more than theory. This is the secret of spiritual victory. Next to justifying faith in a crucified Jesus, as an initial experience, faith in a living, indwelling Christ, always present to impart holy power, and to enable the soul to "overcome," is the fundamental gospel idea. No legal struggles, no desperate resolutions, no intense watchings, no agonizing prayers even, will result in continuous victory. There must be added a peaceful surrender of the soul into the hands of a present Christ, to be kept; with the full faith that he will save it from present spiritual danger and the now urgent temptation. Each one must realize that his or her personal sins, weaknesses, or trials, are perfectly within the scope of Christ's immediate grace; that no besetment is too strong for his conquering arm, at any moment, in any circumstances. No case is so "peculiar," whether from the magnitude or the pettiness of the acts involved, from the eluding brevity or the chronic nature of the trouble, that Christ cannot insure a complete victory "just now." Let us illustrate our meaning by actual experience.

A letter lies before us, addressed, in private correspondence, to a Christian lady, in which is this artless account of the victory gained by a friend of the writer : —

"Mrs. B. has lived for some years in a spirit of entire consecration to God ; but having been carried through months of trial, bereavement, and sickness, she was enabled to drop down, or 'let herself down,' into Jesus so completely, as to be able to testify, moment by moment, 'Jesus saves me, saves me now.' She applied this 'keeping power of Jesus' to each event of life, — to the cares of home-life, the mother's duties, &c. Before this entrance into a life of rest, she had been so tried with servants as to feel at times a longing to die; and her little boy, two and a half years of age, was also a severe trial to her, as he was remarkably wilful. Now one look from her eye reduces the proud spirit to obedience. Recently she had a severe test. A friend said something which wounded her deeply. He knew perfectly what he was saying, and for an instant her spirit rose up against such an outrage. She just lifted her eyes to Jesus, and said, — 'Jesus saves me, saves me now'! Such a flood of joy filled her whole being, that she had to go quickly out of the room, to be alone with God, overpowered with a consciousness of the Holy Spirit's presence."

It is not surprising that the Christian pen which wrote this account added, "Such experiences are so helpful! Do grasp this mighty truth more fully, and present it to those whom you meet. To S—— I gave it, last Saturday, for her nerves. She was miserable, and so unequal to keeping herself! I said, 'When you feel irritable, look up and say, Jesus saves me now from irritable nerves! This has carried her over two days of nervous irritability restfully. Oh, how we grieve Jesus by refusing to believe his promises, — 'He shall be called Jesus; for he shall save his people from their sins.' 'The blood of Jesus Christ cleanseth us from all sin'— as true as they are wonderful! But so few will receive the truth in fulness."

This truth must be more clearly preached from the pulpit, and must be made more thoroughly influential in the experiences of God's people. A present, all-sufficient help is offered ; and this, accepted by faith, insures continuous victory. " This is the victory that overcometh the world, even our faith. Who is he that overcometh the world, but he that believeth that Jesus is the Son of God?"

> " The world and Satan I forsake;
> To thee I all resign :
> My longing heart, O Jesus! take,
> And fill with love divine."

CHAPTER XXII.

CRISES OF THE CAMPAIGN.

THERE is a truth, though one often exaggerated and unwisely employed, in the representations of the "Higher Life" advocates concerning a specific experience, to which they give the names, "Second Conversion," "Baptism of the Holy Ghost," "Perfect Love," and "Christian Perfection." Ideally such a state of spiritual victory and abiding peace is quite distinct from that of legal bondage, moral defeat, and continual despondency. One cannot pass, even in the most cursory reading, from the seventh to the eighth chapters of the Epistle to the Romans, without perceiving a marked change. It is like ascending from the mists of the valley to the clear, bracing atmosphere of the mountain-top. Moreover, these two states usually are chronologically distinct. Ordinarily they are parted by a chasm in the consciousness of the Christian, over which, at a certain definite time, he was borne by the wings of faith. He can look back to a date of deliverance, even as he looks back to the date of his original conversion to God. To others also, as well as to himself, the change then experienced seemed in suddenness, thoroughness, and permanent results, truly to be a second conversion. Christian biography is full of evidence on this point, and the unwritten narratives are still more numerous.

But it is not safe to base on such facts

a definite theory of a state radically separate from that of justification, — a state in all cases subsequently entered, and by an act or process distinct as that by which one passes from the life of an impenitent sinner into that of a Christian. The scriptural evidence in its favor is far from conclusive : indeed, the favorite proof-texts (Eph. i. 13 ; Acts xix. 1–6, and other passages) teach no such idea. The Bible recognizes two separate classes of men on earth: to wit, unconverted sinners, and justified Christians in various stages of sanctification. All the elements of sanctification are found in the justified state. No passage in the New Testament warrants the belief that any man can be justified who does not with his whole heart turn from a life of sin, consecrate himself, body and soul, to God, and trust in Christ as his complete Saviour. This much is involved in the very idea of conversion, or of that "repentance" and "faith" which are made the essential conditions of pardon. But no other *elements* than these enter into the advanced stage of Christian experience. They are simply developed and applied more largely and intelligently, so that single acts become a divinely inspired life, and intermittent exercises grow into an abiding state.

There are some Christians who glide almost imperceptibly into this higher life; some who, born into it at conversion, never need a "second conversion." And we are quite sure that this would oftener be the case, were the instructions given to young converts less legal and more evangelical. What their spiritual necessities require is, that they should go forward from the first moment with as specific a reliance on Christ for adequate and continuous sanctifying grace, as for the pardon of past sin; involving not only equal desire and prayer for the two objects, but *equal expectation*. They should begin with a definite, appropriating faith, rather than with a resolution based on a vague idea of divine aid. The soul's purpose is then implied in the faith, with the advantage, that consciously and chiefly it is a clinging to Christ as an ever-present Saviour, whose grace is each moment all-sufficient. The converts would thus avoid the subsequent declension and experience of legal bondage into which they usually fall. Consequently they would move ever upward, finding each day increasing courage, added joy, easier faith, growing power, and more intimate fellowship with God. Then would be illustrated the declaration: "The path of the just is as the shining light, that shineth more and more unto the perfect day."

But, because such instruction is so seldom or so inadequately given, Christians remain in an infantile state. Instead of gaining wings, or even becoming swift of foot in a race, they do not learn to walk, or indeed hardly to stand. They drop into a life of broken resolutions, constantly renewed and as constantly violated; by which they do indeed persevere in a religious course, but have little spiritual peace, and almost no spiritual power. They have not learned the secret of victory. This gives rise in Christian experience to spiritual crises, in which the soul is lifted into a higher life, after much darkness, sore struggling in prayer, deep heart-searching, and a very intelligent and thorough renewal of consecration and acceptance of Christ. It is the special and powerful work of the Spirit, and therefore is properly called a "baptism of the Holy Ghost." It is a sudden, conscious elevation into a practically new experience, and, therefore, is well enough denominated a "second conversion." It is an enlarged and all-absorbing development of the soul's love to God and Christ, and, therefore, may be termed "perfect love."

This is not a stereotyped experience, which comes with the same incidents in all cases. The crisis with one is the result of quiet private meditation and prayer, with no theory, or expected "state," in mind. With another it is induced by revival preaching, and urgent specific promptings to reach a given experience, which is somewhat technically described. In a third case it follows the discipline of a sore affliction, which darkens earth, but lets in light from heaven. Furthermore, we have reason to think, that, in many persons, there is a series of three or four crises occurring years apart; each caused by some providential event which leads to a life-review, puts the soul on yet deeper self-searching and consecration, and is followed by clearer and more blissful realizations of God. After the attention has been directed to this provision for spiritual need, some attain speedily to the life of gospel liberty, and others slowly; some also rise to it with facility, while others pass through an agonizing struggle. But where true consecration exists, this difference is probably owing to temperament, and to want of clear perception of the office and result of faith; since a similar difference is seen between ordinary converts in a revival.

The way of wisdom, in our view, is to say little of a technical state, but much of *a life of faith in Christ*, which should be described as an abiding experience of purity, peace, and power, such as makes victory characteristic of the soul by the supernatural influence of the indwelling Spirit. Thus there will be found a striking fulfilment of the words of the prophet: " He giveth power to the faint; and to them that have no might he increaseth strength. Even the youths shall faint and be weary, and the young men shall utterly fall; but they that wait upon the Lord shall renew their strength; they shall mount up with wings as eagles; they shall run and not be weary, and they shall walk and not faint."

> " Soul, then know thy full salvation;
> Rise o'er sin and fear and care;
> Try to find, in every station,
> Something still to do or bear;
> Think what Spirit dwells within thee;
> Think what Father's smiles are thine;
> Think that Jesus died to win thee:
> Child of heaven, canst thou repine?"

CHAPTER XXIII.

LEGAL EXPERIENCE A DEFEAT.

THE passage in Rom. vii. 14–25, descriptive of a sore spiritual conflict, has long perplexed the interpreters, who have discussed, in every possible form, the question whether in it the apostle means (either from his own case, or by a figurative personation of the truth), to describe a regenerate or an unregenerate experience. When the dispute has divided the most eminent Greek scholars, the ablest theologians, and the most devout saints, and harmony of view has not yet been secured, we can hardly expect to accomplish much by such brief remarks as can here be offered. Yet as the progress of years has brought us to a settled view, differing from that which we at first held, and in which we were educated; as our conclusion has been maturely tested, not only by exegetical study, but by its spiritual application in Christian training; and as the matter lies in our mind in a somewhat different form from that in which ordinarily it is discussed, we may be pardoned a few suggestions fitted to the comprehension of plain readers of the New Testament.

The interpretation of the passage has been embarrassed by the unnecessary assumption, that it must describe either a regenerate or an unregenerate man. Hence the one class of interpreters have mustered all the possible evidence to show that such and such parts of the experience naturally belong to a converted soul; while the other class have labored as minutely and exhaustively to show that such and such other parts naturally characterize an unconverted soul. But, in form at least, this appears to us to be a false issue. The alternative question, as we should state it, is not: Is this the habitual experience of a Christian, or is it the struggle of an awakened sinner, who is not yet converted? but it is: Is this set forth as a distinctively evangelical experience, or as one of a legal type, in whomsoever it may be found? If this is the real point to be decided, then both classes of interpreters may be partly right and partly wrong; for the passage may describe the experience of a converted man, and one which is but too common in Christians, and yet the experience may be purposely set forth as defective in the evangelical element, as abnormal to a proper Christian state, and as exemplifying the operation of law rather than of gospel in the work of sanctification. And this is our idea of it.

The arguments on both sides have been correspondingly inconclusive. They have hinged too much on single expressions and the contents of the passage itself. Those who were determined to make out the case of a converted man, pointed to the use of "I" and "me," and of the verbs in the present tense, — " I am," " I do," " I allow not," " I consent," " I hate," &c.; as though Paul told of his own state of mind at the time of writing. They further pointed to such strong expressions with reference to sin as "what I hate" and "the evil which I would not;" also to such language respecting holiness as, "what I would," "I delight in the law of God, after the inward man," and "I myself serve the law of God." But, on the contrary side, those who insisted on making out an unconverted man, had their equally strong expressions, which seemed only appropriate to one yet unregenerate and unpardoned; such as, "I am carnal, sold under sin," "sin that dwelleth in me," "how to perform that which is good I find not," "the law of sin which is in my members," "oh, wretched man that I am!" &c. Now, both parties should have remembered, that impersonations and numerous and strong expressions in such a passage, especially in the case of a glowing writer like Paul, are never to be urged as decisive, apart from the general drift of the context. In this case they in a measure balance and neutralize each other; and neither party is convinced by the favorite citations of the other party, because these are susceptible of easy explanation, and are to be taken more rhetorically than logically. But we can claim these very facts in favor of our own view; for the two classes of expressions taken together would seem to show a state of mind which, in respect to conscience, affections, and purpose, may have much which is truly Christian, while yet the experience as a whole, and in result, is sorrowfully legal and weak, rather than joyously evangelical and strong. The gospel offers something better, therefore something more victorious and blissful.

The way is thus cleared to state the three considerations which determine our judgment to this explanation: —

1. The drift and necessities of the apostle's argument in the epistle require such a view. In order to prove the need of the gospel salvation, and its efficacy, he is compelled to demonstrate in the early chapters the universality of human sin and ruin, and the impossibility of justification by the law. Then he brings forward Christ's atoning sacrifice, and the offer of a free pardon to the penitent believer, and defends the scheme from the charge of antinomianism, or of doing away with the need of holiness. All this occupies him nearly to the middle of this seventh chapter, when there remains the important question, Whether the law, though a failure

as to justification, may not suffice as a sanctifying influence, now that our sins are forgiven for Christ's sake? Is Christ as necessary for sanctification as for justification? Does the converted and pardoned soul need him in order to a victorious life, as truly as does the convicted sinner in order to justification? If that be not discussed in this passage, and settled emphatically, against the law, then Paul's argument is plainly incomplete: not only so, but if the experience here given be his own state at the time, and, as it were, the normal and to-be-expected experience of saints in this world, he seems to concede a failure in the gospel. We cannot so interpret him.

2. The passage taken as a whole, apart from single expressions, necessi-

tates the same view. After all that can be urged from words and phrases indicative of a regard for holiness and a dislike of sin, the emphatic and all-significant fact remains, that, from beginning to end, there is nothing of *result* described but utter, habitual, characteristic defeat! Not a note of victory is anywhere heard: only the wail of despair! "Sold under sin;" "what I would that I do not, but what I hate that do I;" "how to perform that which is good I find not;" "the good that I would I do not, but the evil which I would not that I do;" "I find then a law, that when I would do good, evil is present with me;" "I see another law in my members warring against the law of my mind, and bringing me into captivity to the law of sin which is in my members;" "Oh wretched man that I am: who shall deliver me from the body of this death?" Such is not a single expression, but the drift of the whole passage, and even its exclusive declaration, so far as actual *results* are described. The only word of cheer is, when he answers the above despairing question, in a *parenthetical* clause, " I thank God through Jesus Christ, our Lord ;" which he throws in as no part of the state which he is describing, but by way of anticipation of the deliverance which he depicts immediately after, in the next chapter, as the result of another and far higher experience. This unrelieved aspect of defeat shows that Paul writes here of legal failure and not of gospel success.

3. And then this view is corroborated by the purposely contrasted experience,

the description of which immediately follows. The eighth chapter is of entirely opposite tone. It sings, and fairly shouts! It tells only of victory. It cannot possibly mean the same generic experience as the one of lamentation and defeat which has preceded. Both cannot be truly evangelical in character, though both may be found in converted men. It must be Paul's intent to call men out of the first into the second, as the genuine gospel state into which he himself had entered. For, mark this fact: he not only uses the same impersonation, but the expressions in the eighth chapter are specifically chosen to represent the contradiction of the state in the seventh chapter. Thus in the seventh: "I am carnal" (fleshly) and "in me, that is in my flesh, dwelleth no good thing;" but in the eighth: "Who walk not after the flesh, but after the Spirit," and "To be carnally-minded is death, but to be spiritually minded is life and peace." In the seventh: "I see another law . . . bringing me into captivity to the law of sin which is in my members;" "who shall deliver me from the body of this death?" but in the eighth: "The law of the Spirit of life in Christ Jesus hath made me free from the law of sin and death." In the seventh: "Oh wretched man that I am!" but in the eighth, "There is now no condemnation to them who are in Christ Jesus." This contrast of language hardly allows one to think otherwise than that Paul sets forth the legal experience in the seventh chapter, and the evangelical in the eighth.

We cannot but feel that there is a further corroboration of the above interpretation in the more inspiring and hopeful view which it presents of the Christian life. The idea, that the highest type of attainment on earth is after all described in the seventh chapter, is greatly discouraging to the more earnest believers, while it acts as an opiate to the consciences of the worldly minded. This is not the use intentionally made of it by the good men who hold such a view : they apply it rather to the cultivation of humility in some, and the prevention of too great despondency in others, by citing its language as descriptive of Paul's own spiritual condition. Yet practically, and on a large scale, it seems to us a restriction on Christian hope ; and we find great comfort, and a growing sense of power and liberty, in the other view. The church sadly needs lifting, first out of worldliness, and secondly out of legality. Christians must learn that sanctification, as well as justification, is by faith; that spiritual victory is not by natural law, but by grace.

> "My God, I cry, with every breath,
> For some kind power to save,
> To break the yoke of sin and death,
> And thus redeem the slave."

CHAPTER XXIV.

VICTORY OVER PRIDE.

THIS is one of the victories which the saint must win, and it is by no means the easiest. It has been a favorite idea with theologians, preachers, and poets, that pride is the root-sin; that by it the angels fell, and our first parents were led astray in the garden. Nor does it require very ingenious and farfetched reasoning, to give color to that idea, even if it cannot be philosophically established. Selfishness, which is so commonly set forth as the generic form of sin, of which other sins are the species, might be said to involve an overweening estimate of one's own importance, and thus to be only another name for pride. But, however that may be, certain it is that the word of God abounds in warnings in this direction. All are familiar with such texts as these: " Pride goeth before destruction, and a haughty spirit before a fall." " Pride and arrogancy .... do I hate." " Those that walk in pride, he is able to abase." " Out of the heart of men proceed evil thoughts, ... pride, foolishness ; all these evil things come from within and defile the man." " The pride of life is not of the Father." " Not a novice, lest being lifted up with pride, he fall into the condemnation of the Devil," said Paul, with reference to the choice of a pastor. Inculcations of humility as the opposing virtue are on every page of Scripture.

Let us gain a clear idea of the field

upon which this spiritual battle is to be fought, and of the enemy with whom we are to contend. There is a sense in which pride is used to denote a genuine virtue; as when we "take pride" in good qualities, and have such a sense of the debasement of certain evil deeds that we count them beneath us. The natural and proper element of human nature, of which an evil pride is the perversion, is self-esteem. Who can deny that there is a proper estimate for each man to put upon himself,—one which is simply true and just, and which is necessary to efficient action? Can humility be the belief of a lie? Such it would be, did it require us to form an under-estimate of ourselves, quite contrary to fact. In order to be humble, must a skilful mechanic deny his skill, and proclaim or deem himself incompetent? Is it pride for a teacher to think that he is more intelligent than his pupils; or for a parent to assume to be wiser than his children? Humility is not the denial of truth, nor is pride its assertion. We cannot avoid knowing that in certain respects we surpass some other men; and there is no pride in quietly acting upon the knowledge, for necessary purposes.

Pride is cherishing an overestimate of our relative importance, involving a corresponding depreciation of others, accompanied by neglect of them or contempt for them. It is self-worship, and thus a species of idolatry. Humility, on the other hand, is a willingness to pass at our real worth, whatever that may be, —a readiness to take the precise place which God has assigned to us, not envying those who seem to be in a superior position, or despising those below us, or striving to mount higher than God's providence and our own true capacity and usefulness indicate. Inasmuch as men usually decide such points by sheer will, determined to subordinate all they can to their own advancement, and as the best are tempted to overestimate their natural powers, their acquired talents, and their excellence of character, and thus to strive unwisely for high positions, and, in case of failure, to fall into unhappiness and censure of others, the Scriptures properly warn against pride, and urge to a "lowliness of mind," which shall be ready "to esteem others better than themselves." That is, love will be so fearful of unduly depreciating others, and of exalting self, that it will prefer to cherish a high judgment of them, and a low estimate of self. Indeed, when the dangers which throng around pride are realized, — the unloveliness of disposition, the jealousy, the ambition, the disappointments, the unrest, the strife, the hatred, — nothing seems more reasonable than the injunction, "Be not high-minded, but fear."

Adversity tests us in respect to our pride. We may not have suspected it; for it is an insidious sin, and has great skill in putting on virtue's garb, assuming to be only a proper self-respect. But when our plans fail, when our ambitions are frustrated, when we do not gain the position or the praise we have coveted, and lose, perhaps, even that which we have enjoyed, then we awake to the fact that pride has had a strong hold in our heart. It is a time of searching with a Christian, in which he humbles himself before God, and seeks forgiveness for having desired and sought human honor, instead of quietly accepting such position as God might see wise to assign. It is a great victory, to be so much more concerned as to the divine opinion, and to be so fully satisfied to please God and to be used by him, in any capacity, to work out his wise and good will, that little anxiety is felt as to the highness or lowness of our position in the eyes of men. Pride cares for this latter, because it works for self and not for God, and is intent on its own honor rather than on the divine glory.

Hence pride may pervert even actual facts of personal superiority to others, by omitting to trace them to God, and to consecrate them to his service, and by feeding one's self-admiration with them. If the faculties which we possess, and the virtues we acquire, are recognized by us in simplicity of spirit, honestly but humbly, intelligently but lovingly, and are ascribed to divine grace, they will do us no harm in the recognition. But it is dangerous to dwell on such facts of comparison, and Satan will be quite ready to lead the way thither. It is much safer to meditate on our faults and follies, on our errors and sins, and to think how much we need forgiveness for the evil which we have done, and for the good which we have left undone. When pride becomes a self-conceit as to our attainments in holiness, it is sometimes called spiritual pride, and it then falls into the singular contradiction of being proud of one's humility!

The victory over pride will be gained in proportion as we place God above self, and his judgment above human approbation, and exercise such faith in his Fatherly love and wise providence, as to be quite content to take any work or place he chooses to appoint. It is a blessed experience to be so emptied of self-seeking as to be able to say with the Psalmist, "Lord, my heart is not haughty, nor mine eyes lofty; neither do I exercise myself in matters too high for me. Surely I have behaved and quieted myself as a child that is weaned of his mother; my soul is even as a weaned child." Not a little of the "hurt" feeling which many Christians have, is simply wounded pride. A humble soul would have taken no offence, would have perceived no slight, would have missed no commendation.

"Oh, learn that it is only by the lowly
　　The paths of peace are trod!
　If thou wouldst keep thy garments white and holy,
　　Walk humbly with thy God.

" The lowly spirit God hath consecrated
　　As his abiding rest :
　An angel by some patriarch's tent hath waited,
　　When kings had no such guest."

CHAPTER XXV.

VICTORY OVER ANXIETY.

WHO of us has not something of the nature of Martha?—that saint "careful and troubled about many things," and who, probably, was not entirely relieved by the assurance of Jesus, that "but one thing is needful." The human mind is never content with the present, and, in a sense, never ought to be. It was made for progress, and it has knowledge of a future. Therein it differs from lower natures, which live only in the present, taking no note of time, and having no care for the morrow. The bird sings, and the ox grazes, heedless of what is to be. But this marks the inferior order of being. Man leads a higher life, and has the idea of time, past, present, and future. He has foresight and imagination, and, in a measure, can anticipate what is to come. It is a necessity laid upon him, to plan for the future. This is not only the prompting of his natural instincts, and of his individual necessities, but it is a duty imposed by his relations to others, who are dependent upon him, and for whose ever-recurring wants he must provide.

But then foresight, imagination, and plan are apt to develop anxiety. Indeed, it might be asked how anxiety is to be avoided, when the elements of calculation for the future are uncertain, and are largely beyond our individual control? When important results cannot be made sure, how shall a sensitive nature not be anxious until events are determined? And, possibly, it will be claimed that anxiety is reasonable and unavoidable, when disasters plainly impend, and one knows not how to avert them. At such a time all one's personal hopes and fears, all one's love for wife and children, all one's concern for truth, righteousness, and the church of Christ, conspire to create a soul-absorbing anxiety.

And so it happens, that the world is full of anxious men and women; who carry heavy burdens of care, heave deep sighs of solicitude, and gaze earnestly and sadly towards the future. Thoughts of the morrow will not allow them to enjoy to-day. It may be the merchant, apprehensive of the disappointment of his hopes in a business venture; or the laborer, out of employment and with a family to support; or a clerk, likely to lose a situation; or a minister, who, in parish work, fears failure where he looked for success; or a wife, who shares the varying feelings as well as fortunes of her husband; or a mother, who dreads the issue of a child's illness, or the crisis of a son's character; or a sufferer from disease, who anticipates the possibility of years of pain and perhaps of poverty. Sometimes the fact reveals itself in the face; more often it hides in the heart. Neither men nor women tell of their deepest anxieties. They meet others with a smile, and engage pleasantly in the chit-chat of daily life, yet are conscious, the while, of an inward pang, of a dark foreboding, of a torturing fear.

Is there relief from this state of mind?

Can there be, in this respect, a victory for the Christian? Does not anxiety belong to our nature, circumstanced as it now is? If we are "not to boast of to-morrow," because we "know not what a day may bring forth," does it not follow, for the same reason, that we must feel apprehensive as to its possible developments? To such inquiries the Scriptures give a plain answer. They not only promise a spiritual deliverance from this enemy of our peace, but insist that victory is our duty. They also tell us that faith in God is the weapon which secures the victory. What other can be the meaning of Jesus, when he says, "Take, therefore, no thought for the morrow: for the morrow shall take thought for the things of itself. Sufficient unto the day is the evil thereof"?

His reason for this dissuasive from anxious, desponding, brooding thought, is previously expressed, in his argument from God's care of the birds and of the lilies, — which ought to assure us of his greater willingness to provide food and raiment for his children, — and in the direct assertion, "Therefore take no thought, saying, what shall we eat? or what shall we drink? or wherewithal shall we be clothed? (for after all these things do the Gentiles seek:) for your heavenly Father knoweth that ye have need of all these things."

The argument is simply this: we are not left to our own wisdom and strength, in providing for the future ; but we have a heavenly Father, able and willing to supply all our true wants. If we believe this truth, and put firm trust in our

Father, anxiety will necessarily cease. Why are not our children deeply concerned lest next week, or next month, they should not have food and clothing and home? Why do they not move solemnly through the house, or walk thoughtfully along the streets, fearful lest shortly their wants should be unsupplied? Because they have faith in their parents: they believe fully in a mother's love and in a father's ability. It ought not to be a rare attainment in piety, though plainly it is such, to lose one's apprehensions of earthly evil, in the sweet recognition of God's fatherly care. Paul writes, "I would have you without carefulness," — which does not mean without reasonable prudence and precaution, but without a mind full of care, weighed down with forebodings of evil.

In a similar spirit he says, "Be careful for nothing ; but in every thing, by prayer and supplication with thanksgiving, let your requests be made known unto God ; and the peace of God, which passeth all understanding, shall keep your hearts and minds through Christ Jesus."

Even under the Old Testament, faith was the instrument of victory in the conflict with anxiety. Who does not call to mind the Psalmist's words? "Why art thou cast down, O my soul? and why art thou disquieted within me? Hope thou in God; for I shall yet praise him, who is the health of my countenance and my God." And how beautifully the New Testament lays the basis for such faith, in the declaration, " And we know that all things work together for good to them that love God." Yes, "we know" it; but alas! too often we forget it, and, in forgetting it, lose our comfort and our hope, and actually mistake some of God's "good things" for things altogether evil. "All these things are against me," said the patriarch Jacob, in an hour of despondent unbelief. He long since learned better. Anxiety is natural; only, grace is higher than nature! Men of the world, recognizing no Father in heaven, may well be weighed down with care; but of the saint it is said, "Thou wilt keep him in perfect peace, whose mind is stayed on Thee, because he trusteth in Thee. Trust ye in the Lord forever; for in the Lord Jehovah is everlasting strength." And so we may exultingly sing, with Faber, —

"I have no cares, O blessed Will!
  For all my cares are thine:
I live in triumph, Lord, for Thou
  Hast made thy triumphs mine.

"And when it seems no chance or change
  From grief can set me free,
Hope finds its strength in helplessness,
  And gayly waits on thee."

CHAPTER XXVI.

VICTORY OVER SENSITIVENESS.

THAT is a grand attainment, when one reaches the spiritual equilibrium in which the soul appreciates criticism, but is not brought into bondage to it. There can be no improvement without the aid of criticism. Ignorance, habit, and self-esteem blind one to his faults. At first, in every department of action, every one is a novice, and must be taught by the more experienced. He has not sufficient knowledge to understand when he is at fault. The standard of judgment rises with progress in intelligence, with increase of skill. And then that to which one is accustomed wears the aspect of propricty, even though it be sadly defective ; so that sharp criticism by another is needed to startle the mind into a recognition of the truth. And how slow human nature is to admit personal defects, whether of beauty, of strength, of talent, of learning, of taste, or of character! It injures one's self-esteem to be made conscious of errors and defects ; and, as that is an unpleasant frame of mind, it is usually avoided. Self-complacency is a happier state for the time being; though in the end it may bring upon one a rude and even fatal shock. But it hinders progress. As only the consciously sick seek a physician, so only those who recognize their own faults strive to improve. That was a most rational prayer of the Psalmist: "Who can understand his errors? Cleanse thou me from secret faults."

But while we thus need the suggestions of others, to perfect both our character and work, and should not be above learning even from the accusations of our enemies, we cannot easily avoid being sensitive to blame. The good opinion of our fellow-men is justly to be prized. It is a reward for past effort; it is a stimulus to future endeavor. It brings present happiness, and inspires a joyous hope. It strengthens self-respect, and it draws us into the society of those who seem to be pleased with our persons and our character. Blame is therefore repressing in its influence, chilling one's aspirations, and leading him to withdraw from intercourse with others. To some very sensitive souls it comes like an early frost to tender plants, cutting them down ere they have acquired strength and ripe ness. It is natural, then, to shrink from reprehension. When it does not excite anger, it produces grief. If we are wise enough not to give way to resentment, we may yet be weak enough to yield to discouragement.

But sensitiveness is most keen and distressing, when a conviction is felt of the injustice of the blame. To be sharply criticised when one has done well; to have unreal faults pointed out, whether from ignorance or malevolence; to know that genuine talent and skill are unappreciated, and that their reward is grudged; to have motives aspersed, when they have been pure, — that is the trial of trials. To this form of mental suffering our Saviour must have been pre-eminently exposed, for his life was one long conflict with misunderstanding and malice. Nobody properly appreciated him ; not even his disciples ; not even John. And the experience of Paul was similar. No apostle labored so abundantly, or with such self-denial; and none was so misconceived and abused, whether by Jews, Gentiles, or professed Christians. Every saint is put into this furnace, sooner or later, and the flames of it are hot. Many, indeed, furnish part of the fuel by their over-sensitiveness to even the least misconception, as also by a blindness to their own defects, which leads them improperly to impute injustice to the criticisms of others.

There is a spiritual victory, however, to be won upon this very field. Christ had a peace too deep to be disturbed by human censure ; even if it be admitted that he could not but feel a momentary sorrow, when men blamed where they should have praised. And it was because his faith in his Father was so perfect, that he could rise above the influence of human opinion, disregard equally man's plaudits and censures, and, as Peter phrased it, "commit himself to Him who judgeth righteously." And this blissful composure the Saviour imparts to the true believer, in accordance with the assurance, "Peace I leave with you; *my peace* I give unto you." He it was who enabled Paul to overcome his natural sensitiveness in this direction: so that the apostle could say, "With me it is a very small thing that I should be judged of you, or of man's judgment; yea, I judge not my own self. . . . But he that judgeth me is the Lord." A genuine Christian faith refuses to live merely in the present, and to recognize only men. It never loses sight of the glorious hereafter, and of the Master who soon shall say, "Well done, good and faithful servant: enter thou into the joy of thy Lord." Do we not perceive, on reflection, that the painful sensitiveness to human censure, or to a failure to appreciate our efforts, is owing to our undue regard for human opinion? We seek our happiness too much in man's favor. Can we not rise to the experience which enabled the Psalmist to say, "Thou art my portion, O my God." "Whom have I in heaven but thee ; and there is none upon the earth whom I desire besides thee"? In that case we should not live upon the breath of human applause, and die when it was withheld. At best, man is ignorant and is fickle ; he oftentimes condemns when he should approve, and, again, wearying of praise, unjustly censures those who have steadily persevered in good. Let us not make ourselves dependent, then, upon his approbation. If we do not too eagerly expect it, we shall not be overmuch cast down if it be withheld. Jesus warned us against danger on this side, when he said to the opposing Jews, "How can ye believe, who receive honor one of another, and seek not the honor that cometh from God only?" Our victory over sensitiveness to the blame or unappreciativeness of others must come through singleness of aim and simplicity of spirit. Be it our one purpose to please God! Be it joy enough to have the sweet consciousness that such is our intent, and the quiet assurance, that, in so living, he accepts us in Christ!

"O Lord, I cast my care on thee;
   I triumph and adore.
Henceforth my great concern shall be
   To love and please thee more."

CHAPTER XXVII.

VICTORY IN DETAIL.

A TRUE soldier obeys orders in the minutest particular. Military life subjects every thing to control. How shall the Christian know that he is carrying out the will of his commander in the details of life? The New Testament contains a passage, familiar to Christian ears, which concisely states the true rule of action in these words: "Whether, therefore, ye eat or drink, or whatsoever ye do, do all to the glory of God." This seems to be a sufficiently simple direction, and yet not a few have been puzzled by it. The practical difficulty has been, to keep this motive always in mind ; to bethink one's self of the divine glory in connection with the thousand shifting circumstances of life, which develop feeling and require numerous decissions on subordinate grounds. Ministers have sometimes preached, or have been understood to preach, to the great confusion of mind of their hearers, that, the only reason for action being the glory of God, no one ought to take pleasure in an amusement, or to enjoy an article of food, because of any attractive quality in it. To play ball from any love of the sport, or to eat a dish of oysters from any relish for the food, is said to be sinful : the act must be done only for the glory of God. "But," say many conscientious souls, in sore trouble under such seemingly harsh and impracticable directions, "we find that these acts are instinctive, and we perform them in response to natural desires and tastes, without pausing each time to summon up a distinct motive connected with the divine glory. We sincerely mean to live for God in all respects, and to avoid whatever he forbids; and yet sometimes busy hours pass with no distinct thought of God in the mind. What are we to do?"

The language of the preachers referred to is not happy, even if their meaning be in the main correct. It were better, did they say that no act should be performed from any motive which is not subordinated to the purpose to do all things to the glory of God. A distinction should be drawn between generic and specific motive. A young man in Chicago learns that his father is ill in Massachusetts, and starts immediately to see him. The generic reason or motive for the journey is found in love for his father. This really leads to every act necessary to reach his bedside,—the packing of a trunk, the purchase of a ticket, the stepping into the car, the persistent riding in it for two days, &c. Nevertheless, it is quite possible, that during those two days, for an hour at a time he may not think of his father, while he is reading a book or a newspaper, or is gazing at the scenery, or is in conversation with his fellow travellers. So also he will not directly connect with his father his enjoyment of the meals by the way, and many other incidental facts. Yet it is plain, that deep in the soul, below all these specific acts with their particular motives, lies the comprehensive, determining purpose to go to his father. So in the case of another young man, in the same car, who is on his way to college to gain an education. In one sense, he rides, he eats, he sleeps, because it is pleasant to go to a certain place, to satisfy hunger, and to refresh a weary body; but, in a higher sense, he does all these as means to carry out his grand purpose to be educated.

When Jefferson Davis became a traitor to his country, and the head of the rebellion, his main political purpose was corrupt; and this imparted a taint of treason to all his acts. His life was devoted to disloyal aims; and thus his walking and riding, his eating and sleeping, his reading and writing, were but parts of a permanent purpose of rebellion, and however harmless as isolated acts, and whatever he might be thinking about at the moment, were guilty as related to the unworthy object to which he had devoted himself. In like manner, Abraham Lincoln was serving his country, not only when he was holding cabinet consultations, or visiting the camps, or writing messages to Congress, but in all his deeds, from putting on his clothes in the morning to the taking them off at night. And if, at certain hours, he walked or rode for recreation, or enjoyed a dinner or a lively conversation with his friends, neither the act, nor his enjoyment of it, was at all inconsistent with his patriotism ; for that virtue covered his entire life.

This will enable us to understand that a Christian may honestly consecrate his life to God, and purpose to do all things to the divine glory, and yet not literally be thinking of God each moment, or be consciously raising a question about the divine glory in each specific act. An honest, generic motive thus to live will naturally underlie and shape the details of life as they occur, and will not be in the least degree inconsistent with such enjoyment as naturally pertains to them. For did not God benevolently create our natural desires, and provide objects to gratify them? Does not his glory require, on the one hand, that our entire nature should be developed, and, on the other, that all his gifts should be gratefully and joyfully appropriated?

A wise and benevolent teacher says to his faithful scholars, "Take to-morrow as a holiday: you have studied well for many weeks, and now I want you to have

a good time. Nothing will please me
more than to see you happy at your
games all the day." It will be no dishonor to the teacher, should the scholars
during that holiday not once think of
their studies, and only remember him for
the moment, as the kind bestower of that
season of sport. He will not question
them, the day after, to know whether
they paused before each bat-stroke to
recall his memory; or whether they took
delight in playing ball because they
liked the game, or only because they
wished to honor him. There would be
no incompatibility between the two
things. A mechanic may take great
pleasure in his work for its own sake;
and yet his aim may be to please his
employer, or to earn money with which
to support his family. An artist may

delight in art for its own charm, and yet pursue it as the vocation to which God calls him.

The Scriptures mean that we shall honestly seek to please God in our whole lives. That purpose may underlie our conduct, shaping all that we do, even though for hours it come not directly into consciousness. A Christian student none the less acts for the glory of God, because he cannot think of him in the midst of an algebraic process or of a geometrical demonstration. He may glorify him also in his amusements; though he enjoy the amusement for its own sake, while yet employing it as a needed recreation for subsequent study. What God wants is a spirit of consecration, of joy, of gratitude; that we shall sincerely mean to please him by our manner of life at all times. Thus will our spiritual victory be carried into the minutest details of life, "casting down imaginations and every high thing that exalteth itself against the knowledge of God, and bringing into captivity every thought to the obedience of Christ."

> "Oh that every deed and word
>   May proclaim how good thou art!
> Holiness unto the Lord,
>   Now be written on each heart."

CHAPTER XXVIII.

VICTORY ON THE FIELD OF BUSINESS.

SPIRITUAL victory must be won precisely where the providence of God may choose to order the battle. The saint cannot choose his battle-field, except in a very limited way; as when he avoids dangerous temptations which no duty requires him directly to face, and which prudence and self-knowledge tell him it would be presumption and not faith to encounter. As God orders our lot from day to day, when we trust ourselves to his care, so he assigns, incidentally, the times and places of conflict. At each such time and place we may expect his presence and help, and may gird ourselves with courage and hope for the conflict.

Perhaps the most common and dangerous battle is that waged on the field of secular business. There Satan has strongly intrenched himself. There his forces are numerous, and his natural advantages great. Having ruled in this realm with small interruption, he has arranged the usages and maxims of business to favor the principle of self-pleasing, and to rule out God. And yet the Christian may not pass around this battle-field. His way lies directly across it, at whatever hazard. Industry is the law of life. Work is duty; and work must be located by human necessities, not by our desires. And so a saint must be such in the shop, the store, the office, as well as in the church edifice. In fact, his saintship must vindicate itself conspicuously in secular affairs, in order to prove its health, its robustness, its very reality. Failure in that sphere would be fatal; for it would be failure in the place where the larger part of one's life must be spent, and where the great mass of men must have their moral conflict.

It would never answer to have piety associated only with the life of a recluse, — a hermit, a monk, a scholar in his study, — or even with that of a clergyman devoted wholly to spiritual thought and work. The appearance would be as if religion were not meant to be the common inheritance and joy of the whole human family, but to be the possession of a few privileged characters. It might seem as if God could not save from all sin, but only from some sins. In the old wars of Israel with the heathen, the latter, it will be remembered, imagined at one time that Jehovah was a God of the hills, and could give success to his people only in a mountain-fight, but had no power to help on the plain. It would wear that semblance, surely, in the spiritual conflict, if God's grace triumphed in the hill-region of churches, but not in the plain-country of secular business, — if it could make holy monks, priests, ministers, but not holy laborers and mechanics, holy merchants and physicians, holy lawyers and statesmen.

The Bible teaches that piety is equally to characterize all classes, of whatever rank or occupation. Its representative saints were seldom men of seclusion.

Elijah and John the Baptist were such, to fit them for a special mission; but usually the holy men of old were shepherds, agriculturists, warriors, kings, statesmen, and men of other busy secular occupations; as the very names of Abraham, Isaac, Jacob, Joseph, Joshua, David, Nehemiah, and Daniel will suggest. Go back even to the life of Enoch, who is so eminent in holy character as having "walked with God," and the brief biography before his glorious translation implies that he was no recluse. His was not a celibate saintship, or a piety nurtured in privacy; as is seen from the simple fact that he was a man of family, and "begat sons and daughters." Of course he needed to labor industriously for their support; and he was able to do this, and yet maintain a consistent walk with God, and that amid prevailing wickedness. So faith must be compatible with pursuing a secular calling, and the victories which it wins in that sphere will be of special honor to religion. Men of the world will admit that a clergyman may be a consistent saint, because they think (quite mistakenly) that his spiritual occupation exempts him from temptation, and almost necessitates godliness. But they doubt the value and power of divine grace amid the selfishness and corruption of business life. Hence nothing can be so impressive as the example of a devoted Christian who is also successful in secular affairs. How shall this victory be won?

First of all, consecration to God must be as complete in a business-Christian as in a minister. He must go into business for the same reason that the minister preaches the gospel; to wit, that God has called him to that life-work. He is to accept his business as the sphere in which to be holy and useful. He must not take a merely selfish view of it, as though it were only a means of getting a livelihood, regarding it as an ox views a pasture-ground. He must not make it a tool of personal ambition, hoping to become wealthy and influential. He acts for God in his sphere, as the clergyman does in his. Both should have one spirit, and are under the same law to Christ. This idea kept in mind will be a perpetual safeguard. It will lead to industry, honesty, truthfulness; it will save from the reckless gambling spirit; it will induce generosity in the

ON THE FIELD OF BUSINESS. 291

use of property for charitable purposes. No man can consciously do business for God and not find it a means of grace; for, in so doing, he is acting upon the very precept of the apostle: "Whether, therefore, ye eat or drink, or whatsoever ye do, do all to the glory of God."

God's special blessing must be sought continually in connection with business cares and labors. Faith must make its appeal to the heavenly Father, to keep the soul amid the many and powerful temptations which are found in all the walks of secular life. Recourse must be had to the sympathy and aid of that Jesus who for thirty years quietly followed the occupation of a carpenter, and who well knows the trials which belong to the poor in their struggles to obtain the necessaries of life. As nothing is more regular than business, claiming as it does steady attention for many hours each day, so the Christian must be regular in seeking divine help for the discharge of its many duties. His closet must witness daily supplication for the needed grace, and often must an ejaculatory prayer go up at the very moment of temptation. And no petition has more reason for faith in a favorable answer, since God must surely care for that which occupies so large a part of the lives of his people. There will come also special occasions of trial, when the man of business will be at his wit's end, and when God only can help and give peace amid crushing burdens of responsibility and inrushing tides of anxiety. These are the times when Satan presses upon the soul for its overthrow, suggesting plans of evil and doubts of God's good providence, and when the soul must consequently draw very near to God, and cast itself unconditionally upon the promises.

And, in addition to these specific requests, the Christian must balance the worldly tendencies of business pursuits by a careful use of the means of grace. If his business presses, he is the last man that should neglect family worship or the weekly prayer-meeting. He must hold on to the invisible world by all possible means, and must keep open the channels by which spiritual influences flow in upon the heart. And this is the more evident, when we remember that the business is really God's business, in which he must be constantly consulted; and that he is too reasonable and just to require of us such a supreme devotion to it as shall conflict with the duty and privilege of prayer in the family, or of attendance at the church-meetings. The Bible must be the business man's daily counsellor. Some form of Christian work in the church or Sunday school will aid in the same direction. Through such means he will preserve the tone of his mind amid the excitement of secular life, and will live in a true sense for two worlds. So taught Wesley in his "Working-Hymn:" —

> "Son of the carpenter, receive
> This humble work of mine;
> Worth to my meanest labor give,
> By joining it to thine.
>
> "Thy bright example I pursue;
> To thee in all things rise;
> And all I think or speak or do
> Is one great sacrifice.

"Careless through outward cares I go,
From all distraction free:
My hands are but engaged below,
My heart is still with thee."

CHAPTER XXIX.

VICTORY ACCORDING TO LAW.

IT has been abundantly shown by all that has been said in the foregoing chapters of this book, that spiritual victory is not possible to us under merely legal influences. The law operates, in the case of a fallen nature, to reveal duty, and, at the same time, to condemn for the failure to perform it. It arouses the conscience to an increased sense of sin, but brings no proffer of aid in the conflict. It tells the man of the victory which he should have gained; it mortifies him by an unsparing exposure of his defeat; it places in clear view his responsibility and his moral weakness;

but it utters no word of hope, brings to bear no fresh motive, and has no promise of divine aid. The gospel alone meets the exigency by its new revelation of God in Christ, and by its gracious invitations and pledges, even as Paul declares, " For (what the law could not do, in that it was weak through the flesh), God sending his own Son in the likeness of sinful flesh, condemned sin in the flesh ; that the righteousness of the law might be fulfilled in us who walk not after the flesh, but after the Spirit."

But these very words prove, that while the victory cannot be by the law, it yet must be according to the law ; that is, precisely the same result in character must be secured which the law aimed to secure. The method is changed, not the end. Holiness is immutable. God must require it, whether under a legal or under a gracious economy. There can be no real victory but in subduing whatever is contrary to the will of God as expressed in his eternal law of love, which is the transcript of his own nature. No soldier in war, however valiant he may appear, fights to the acceptance of his general, who does not conform to the rules of military discipline, and whose every act does not aid in reaching the result for which the campaign is planned. The apostle brings out the same idea, when, referring to the contests in the Grecian games, he says, "And if a man also strive for masteries, yet is he not crowned, except he strive lawfully," or according to the rules laid down for the combatants. Our spiritual victory must then be one in the way which God appoints. Yet there are those who imagine that attainment to a perfect state changes the relation of believers to the moral law, so that it is no longer the rule of conduct, the universal standard of right. Thus we hear of "Antinomian Perfectionists," in our own times, and of similarly characterized mystics in the middle ages.

In every age of the church there has been a tendency to "turn the grace of God into lasciviousness," and to "use liberty for an occasion to the flesh." In escaping from bondage to the Mosaic law, early believers were tempted to think that there was no Christian law. When Paul said, "Ye are not under the law, but under grace," and "If ye be led of the Spirit, ye are not under the law," they imagined, in some cases, not only that they could not be justified by the law, but also that no rule of holy living now remained. This brought out earnest protests from that apostle, who wrote, "Do we then make void the law, through faith? God forbid; yea, we establish the law;" and James thought it necessary to argue that there was an obvious sense in which "justification" could not be separated from "works." These Antinomian tendencies, which set law and gospel in antagonism, are always lurking around the subject of salvation by grace. As if there could be any salvation which did not save from sin! As if the very object of divine grace were not *to regenerate and perfect character!* As if pardon were not always conditioned upon repentance as well as upon faith, and as if it did not constitute an additional motive to purity! Yet how often men rest securely in sin, in the expectation that their belief that Christ died for them, and will by his grace save them, would avail to bring his merit to bear for their justification!

But holiness cannot change its nature under any dispensation; nor can that be a true gospel which does not distinctly recognize the one unalterable law of duty. The central idea of the divine law is love; and what a wise love for all beings in their various wants and relationships requires of us in this life, God indicates in the specific precepts of the Bible. He also directs, in his Word, as to the outward means to be used in our condition of weakness and danger, to nourish the principle of love, to avail ourselves of the promised aid of the

Holy Spirit, and to strengthen our faith in Christ as our Example, our Teacher, and our Redeemer. These are such exercises as prayer in secret and in public, the use of psalms and hymns, attendance upon worship and the ministry of the Word, the study of the Scriptures, the celebration of ordinances, the observance of the Lord's Day, and engagement in labors of love for the bodies and souls of our fellow-men. All who imagine that they have come into a spiritual state which absolves from the duty, or relieves from the necessity, of carefully attending to these things, are deluded. They are assuming to be holy without holiness; to be living righteous lives, without any standard of right; to be maintaining a spiritual life, without using the means which God declares to be essential ; to be enjoying a victory, when the enemy is in the field in full force, and when they are not even armed with the weapons needful to resist his attack !

> " Who keepeth not God's word, yet saith,
>   I know the Lord, is wrong :
> In him is not that blessed faith
>   Through which the truth is strong ;
> But he who hears and keeps the word,
>   Is not of this world, but of God."

CHAPTER XXX.

THE FINAL VICTORY.

THERE is a last conflict, and so there is to the Christian a final victory. When the battle has been gained in the fight with the allied forces, — the world, the flesh, and the devil; when our tried, tempest-tossed human nature has found the peace and rest of faith in the Lord Jesus; and when the days, months and years have been spent in such doing and enduring as our heavenly Father may have appointed, — then comes the closing struggle. "The last enemy that shall be destroyed is death," says the received English version; but the original words are more terse: "The

last enemy shall be destroyed, — Death."
We must face him when we have overcome all other foes. There he stands, to the natural eye grim and frightful! How terrible in all ages he has seemed to poor mortals! No one can escape the conflict; for he strides, a giant, across our path, just at its end. Men usually turn pale when they see him, even at a distance; and, in the close grapple, by what terror they are often overcome! This is not unnatural, in certain aspects of the case. Life must shrink from death, the negation of itself, the termination of its happy experiences, the interruption of its plans, the disappointment of its hopes, the sundering of its tenderest ties. And, in a spiritual view, a sinful life cannot calmly contemplate a divine judgment tc which Death

is felt to be related as the officer who drags the criminal before the tribunal of justice. And so men dread to die, and experience a struggle in preparing for the inevitable event.

But on this, as on every other field, Christ is victor. The dawn of each Lord's Day assures us of this fact. It brings the Christian festival, — the Sunday, the day of light, of joy, of hope, because the day of triumph. On "the first day of the week" it was, that the dead Jesus became the living Christ. Death could not hold him in its icy embrace, could not bind him with its iron chains. He submitted to its power, on the cross, because he was a voluntary sacrifice for the world's sin ; now he asserted his divine prerogative, rose in triumph, and dragged Death as a captive behind his car. And this victory was for his people as truly as for himself. He rose as the type and pledge of their resurrection; and faith in this fact lifts them above the fear of death. Admirably is this set forth in the Epistle to the Hebrews : " Forasmuch, then, as the children are partakers of flesh and blood, he also himself likewise took part of the same, that through death he might destroy him that had the power of death, that is, the devil; and deliver them who through fear of death were all their lifetime subject to bondage." And how bold Paul is, speaking of " our Saviour Jesus Christ, who hath abolished death, and hath brought life and immortality to light through the gospel!" This was his habitual feeling. He carried it about in his own breast. He inspired others with it. He claimed that in Christ was fulfilled the prophecy: "Death is swallowed up in victory." He challenges contradiction, and, as it were, taunts the old enemy with his weakness: "O Death, where is thy sting? O Grave, where is thy victory?" He fairly shouts in his exultation: "Thanks be unto God, who giveth us the victory through our Lord Jesus Christ." Nor was this mere theory, or empty rhetoric, with him. He could affirm, "For me to live is Christ, and to die is gain. . . . having a desire to depart, and to be with Christ, which is far better." He could say in the face of persecution, "I am ready not to be bound only, but also to die at Jerusalem, for the name of the Lord Jesus." And when in prison at Rome, awaiting martyrdom, the victor apostle exclaimed, "I am now ready to be offered, and the time of my departure is at hand. I have fought a good fight, I have finished my course, I have kept the faith. Henceforth there is laid up for me a crown of righteousness, which the Lord, the righteous Judge, shall give me at that day; and not to me only, but unto them also that love his appearing." Yes, Paul was in sober earnest when he dared to say that Christ had "abolished death," madman as he must have seemed to all but the little band of believers.

And now eighteen centuries have been accumulating their evidence to the same effect. The disciples of Jesus have gained great victories on this battle-field. Their last enemy has come upon them in many different ways and forms; but, while destroying the body, he has had no power over the soul. He has drawn near gradually, and tried to make himself a terror for long months and years. He has come suddenly, to take the saint unawares, and to crush him with a single stroke. He has appeared as flood, as flame, as axe, as halter, as famine, as pestilence. It was in vain: defeat awaited him. Jesus was always at hand to protect his loved ones. With his sweet word of promise sounding in the ear, the rack itself was a bed of roses, the flames about the stake a chariot of fire for the ascending soul, and the crushing stones could only force from the dying lips the prayer, "Lord Jesus, receive my spirit." Ever since Jesus went before us through the dark valley, it has resounded with the triumphant songs of those who hear his voice, saying, "I am the resurrection and the life; he that believeth in me, though he were dead, yet shall he live; and whosoever liveth and believeth in me shall never die." And so we shall reach the heavenly Canaan and the New Jerusalem, victors to the last!

"There is the throne of David;
And there, from toil released,
The shout of them that triumph,
The song of them that feast;
And they beneath their Leader,
Who conquered in the fight,
Forever and forever
Are clad in robes of white."